CELPIP Vocabulary Practice, Levels 10+:

Hundreds of Key Words, Phrases, and Expressions

Jackie Bolen

www.eslspeaking.org

Table of Contents

About the Author: Jackie Bolen

I taught English in South Korea for 10 years to every level and type of student. I've taught every age from kindergarten kids to adults. Most of my time has centered around teaching at two universities in Cheonan and Busan. These days, I'm teaching teenagers and adults in Vancouver, Canada. In my spare time, you can usually find me outside surfing, biking, hiking, or snowshoeing.

In case you were wondering what my academic qualifications are, I hold a Master of Arts in Psychology. During my time in Korea I successfully completed both the Cambridge CELTA and DELTA certification programs. With the combination of almost 15 years teaching ESL/EFL learners of all ages and levels, and the more formal teaching qualifications I've obtained, I have a solid foundation on which to offer advice to English learners. You can find me here:

YouTube: www.youtube.com/c/jackiebolen

Pinterest: www.pinterest.com/eslspeaking

Email: jb.business.online@gmail.com

You may also want to check out these other books by Jackie Bolen. It's easy to find them wherever you like to buy books.

- English Collocations in Dialogue

- Advanced English Conversation Dialogues

- 1001 English Expressions and Phrases

How to Use this Book

This book is designed to help you build a bigger vocabulary, which is essential for the CELPIP exam. If you want to get a high score on this exam, it will be necessary to know this kind of language.

To use this book, I recommend doing one lesson per day, instead of all of them at one time. This will help you to remember the material. Do the practice exercises, and try not to cheat by looking at the answers!

Use a vocabulary notebook, and be sure to write down any new words that you learn. Review them frequently and consider making some flashcards. Push yourself to use this new vocabulary when speaking and see if you can find them when watching English TV or movies, or reading.

Make sure you know how to pronounce any new word that you learn. Look on YouTube or Google, "How to say _____" to find out. This will help you get a higher score on the speaking section.

This book is one way to expand your vocabulary range. You might also consider extensive reading and listening as well. Find things to listen to (podcasts, movies, TV shows) or read (books, magazine, newspaper articles) that are at your level, or just slightly below. The key is to read or listen just for fun and to not have to use a dictionary all the time. This will not only help you become more familiar with English vocabulary but it'll also help you improve your grammatical accuracy as well.

Be sure to do some practice tests (search on Google for "CELPIP practice test") and record yourself for the speaking section to review later. Try to use the new vocabulary that you've acquired in this book.

Top 10 Tips to Prepare for the CELPIP Exam

If you want to get a high score on the CELPIP exam, here are some tips to pay attention to.

#1: Learn the Test Format

Knowing what to expect on test day is key to getting a high score. Familiarize yourself by looking online for some practice tests. Better yet, consider taking a CELPIP prep class with an experienced teacher.

#2: Know Which Test You're Taking

The CELPIP general is the longer one that covers reading, writing, listening, and speaking. It's a bit more expensive. The CELPIP LS only has listening and speaking, and is a bit cheaper. Double (triple!!) check which one your organization or immigration application requires.

#3: Practice Focusing for 2-3 Hours at a Time

This test takes a long time—3 hours for the CELPIP general, and 1 hour for the general LS. Put your phone away and practice studying for a long period of time, without taking breaks. Get used to focusing for hours.

#4: Eat Breakfast and Get a Good Sleep

Make sure you're at your best for the exam. Get enough sleep the night before. It's a waste of time to "cram" and "pull an all-nighter!" It's best to be sharp and focused. Make sure to eat a good, healthy breakfast beforehand.

Bring a small snack to eat during the short breaks. Wear a t-shirt and bring a sweater along with you. This way, you can adapt to a hot or cold room and remain comfortable.

Arrive on time! For this test, it's 45 minutes early. If you are late, you won't be able to do the test, and you won't get a refund.

#5: Improve your English Typing Skills

You may be proficient at typing on a keyboard in your first language, but what about in English? If you're doing the computer-based exam, this is a key factor. Make sure to do an online tutorial to improve your speed and accuracy.

If you're doing the paper based exam, be sure to bring sharpened pencils, an eraser, and a selection of nice pens.

#6: Practice Taking Notes

Note taking is a key skill for college students. It's also allowed on the CELPIP exam and can be helpful in getting a high score, so get some practice with it. Whenever you listen to, or read something, be sure to take some notes. Create your own shorthand for common words. For example, I use a triangle for "change." I also make frequent use of an equal sign, or an equal sign with a line through it to represent things like equal, similar, same, different, unequal, etc.

#7: Answer Every Single Question

On a multiple choice test with 4 questions, you have a 25% chance of randomly guessing the right answer. However, the good news is that there are usually 1 or 2 answers that are obviously not correct. Eliminate 1 of them, and you have a 33% chance. Eliminate 2, and you have a 50% chance of getting it right.

All that to say, never leave blanks on this exam. Answer every single question. Try to eliminate some answers, if possible, and then make your best guess. For the speaking and writing portions, just say or write something. You will get partial points.

Some topics may be unfamiliar to you. This is normal! Don't panic. The more difficult topics are to separate the very advanced people from the advanced people.

#8: Practice Writing with a Time Limit

Are you one of those people who carefully choose every word that you write in English? Maybe you ponder over whether or not your sentence is grammatically perfect? This is a bad habit that you need to break for the CELPIP exam. There is a strict time limit,

8

and you won't finish the tasks if you do this.

Look up some writing practice tests for the CELPIP online. Follow the time limits. I recommend spending a short time thinking about the points you want to cover and making some brief notes about that (1-2 minutes per section). Then, start writing. Allow 2-3 minutes for proofreading at the end to check for any mistakes. Get used to doing this during your practice sessions, and you'll ace the exam.

#9: Make a Study Plan

You will have to spend a significant amount of time preparing for this exam if you want to get a high score. I don't want to lie about that! The best thing to do is to start around 6 months before. Make a study plan. Include a mix of all four skills, along with studying English vocabulary. Learn about the test format and do practice exams. When the test day comes, you'll be able to feel confident that you've put your best effort in!

#10: Choose a Test Date Wisely

Maybe you're doing the CELPIP to apply for a college or university? Or you want to move to Canada at a certain time. Don't plan to get your results only a few days before the deadline. What if your score isn't high enough? You won't have time to study more, retake the test, and wait for your results.

Instead, I recommend doing the first attempt 6-8 months before the application deadline. If you do well, that's great! If you don't, then you still have 3-4 more months to study, retake the test, and submit your application. This is the stress-free way!

Making Waves

Jerry and Linda are talking about a situation at work.

Jerry: I don't want to **make waves** here, but I don't think Kim is making a good financial decision for our company.

Linda*:* Oh, I don't know. Maybe you just don't see **eye to eye**? I think she's done a lot of research and **knows what she's doing**. She's generally quite good at making decisions. It's why they pay her the **big bucks**.

Jerry*:* Well, I understand why you'd think that. You were **born with a silver spoon in your mouth**, just like Kim, and have never really been **short on cash.** Anyway, it's some **food for thought!**

Linda*:* To play the **Devil's advocate**, making big decisions is **second nature** to her. She's great at it!

Jerry*:* Hmmm...okay. Let's **agree to disagree**. We're never going to **settle** this I think.

Vocabulary

see eye to eye: Agree with someone.

born with a silver spoon in your mouth: Someone who comes from a wealthy family who doesn't have to work that hard in life.

food for thought: Something to think about.

make waves: To cause trouble.

devil's advocate: Someone who takes the other side in an argument.

knows what she's doing: Sure of something or do something correctly.

agree to disagree: To stop talking about something controversial when you can't agree.

settle: Decide or agree to something.

big bucks: To have a very high salary.

second nature: Something that someone does easily and well because they have done it so often.

Practice

1. My mom and I had to finally _____ because there was no way we could understand each other's point of view.

2. I'm not trying to _____ but I just don't agree with what's going on at my company.

3. I'm thinking about changing jobs. My boss and I don't _____.

4. My cousin was _____ and has never had to work a day in his life.

5. My younger brother's most annoying habit is his need to always play the _____.

6. That newspaper article had some _____ in it.

7. I've learned so much from my teacher. I can see she _____.

8. I was hoping to not have to _____ for that job because the salary isn't great but it's tough in this economy.

9. Skating is _____ to him. He's been doing it since he was three.

10. He has a ton of responsibility but that's why they pay him the _____.

Answers

1. agree to disagree

2. make waves

3. see eye to eye

4. born with a silver spoon in his mouth

5. Devil's advocate

6. food for thought

7. knows what she's doing

8. settle

9. second nature

10. big bucks

Wasting Time

Kim and Sally are talking about summer vacation plans.

Kim: What are you up to **this summer vacation**?

Sally: Oh, every summer, we head to our cabin at Lake Minnewanka.

Kim: Wow! I didn't know you had a cabin there.

Sally: Yeah, we bought it **5 years ago** and **since then**, have spent **as much time as possible** there. It's the perfect place for **wasting time**, doing almost nothing.

Kim: Well, you need to make time to relax, right? That sounds **idyllic.**

Sally: Definitely.

Kim: When are you heading out?

Sally: Actually, the **day after tomorrow**. I'm **under the gun** for packing!

Kim: Okay, have an awesome trip! Don't forget about your old friends **slaving away** at work.

Vocabulary

this summer vacation: Usually refers to time off that people have from school or work during July or August (in North America).

5 years ago: Now is 2021. 5 years ago = 2016.

since then: After a certain point in the past.

as much time as possible: The maximum amount, taking into account restrictions like school or work.

wasting time: Not doing much.

idyllic: Tranquil; peaceful.

day after tomorrow: In 2 days. For example, today is Monday. Day after tomorrow = Wednesday.

under the gun: Feeling pressure, usually due to a time constraint.

slaving away: Working hard.

Practice

1. _____, I've been doing way better.

2. I'm going to Japan the _____.

3. I've been _____ on this project for months now.

4. I graduated from high school _____.

5. _____ is what summer vacation is all about!

6. Let's find somewhere _____ to go to for vacation.

7. Can you stay late tonight? We're kind of _____ here.

8. _____, I'd love to finally read those books that have been sitting on my nightstand for months!

9. I try to spend _____ outside. It's great for my mental health.

Answers

1. since then

2. day after tomorrow

3. slaving away

4. 5 years ago

5. wasting time

6. idyllic

7. under the gun

8. this summer vacation

9. as much time as possible

Running a Marathon

Jerry is talking to his friend Linda about running a marathon.

Jerry: I'm thinking about running a marathon. I have **butterflies in my stomach** though. It's going to be difficult!

Linda: What? It'll be **a piece of cake** for you. You're **as fit as a fiddle**.

Jerry: I know I'm always **cool as a cucumber** when I start the race but then I get so tired in the middle. I eventually get a **second wind** though.

Linda: **Fingers crossed** that you'll **knock 'em dead**. I'll come to cheer for you!

Jerry: What about you? Did the doctor give you **a clean bill of health**? You can train with me.

Linda: I'm not quite **back on my feet** yet. Plus, I have **a lot on my plate** right now. I've been **working day and night** on this latest project. I need **a change of pace** for sure!

Vocabulary

a piece of cake: Something that's easy to do.

cool as a cucumber: Very calm or relaxed.

as fit as a fiddle: In really good shape.

second wind: Having some energy again after being tired. Usually applies to exercise or staying up late.

butterflies in my stomach: Nervous feeling about something.

fingers crossed: To wish someone good luck. Or, a symbol of good luck.

knock 'em dead: Do well or be successful at an event.

a clean bill of health: Healthy, not sick anymore.

back on my feet: Recovered, after a problem (health, financial, divorce, etc.)

a lot on my plate: Many responsibilities.

working day and night: Working all the time.

a change of pace: Something new or different.

Practice

1. Don't worry, I'm sure you'll _____.

2. Under pressure, Roger Federer is as _____.

3. I always get _____ before a test.

4. That speaking test was _____.

5. I've got my _____ waiting for the results of the SAT.

6. My grandpa is _____ even though he is 80.

7. My wife has been _____ to get the latest project done at work.

8. I hope I get my _____. I have lots more studying to do!

9. I'm hoping to get _____ after my recent job loss.

10. I'm moving to Costa Rica for _____.

11. I'm hoping that the doctors give me _____.

12. I'm going to have _____ this week at work.

Answers

1. knock 'em dead

2. cool as a cucumber

3. butterflies in my stomach

4. a piece of cake

5. fingers crossed

6. as fit as a fiddle

7. working day and night

8. second wind

9. back on my feet

10. a change of pace

11. a clean bill of health

12. a lot of my plate

Beef Up

Tim and Nathan are talking about cybersecurity at their company.

Tim: I think we need to **beef up** our cybersecurity. We're starting to **fall behind,** and I'm nervous we might **end up** getting hacked.

Nathan: I agree. It's time to **break out** all the tools. I'd rather do some prevention now if it means we don't have to **fight back** against some unknown enemy later.

Tim: I agree. Let's **get it over with**. We have to do it at some point and better late than never.

Nathan: For sure. But, we can't get **carried away** with it. We still have to **stay within** the budget. Let's **hit up** Tony and see what he thinks about this. He's the head of security here.

Vocabulary

beef up: Increase.

fall behind: Not keep up with others.

end up: To be in a place that was not planned for in the end.

break out: Deploy or start to use something.

fight back: Counterattack in a fight or battle.

get it over with: Do something that you don't want to do.

carried away: Do something to an excessive degree.

stay within: Not go over budget or time; not exceed some limit.

hit up: Ask someone for something, usually a favour.

Practice

1. We need to _____ the schedule time for this meeting. I have a dentist appointment after it.

2. I don't want to _____ being stuck next to him at lunch.

3. We're starting to _____ on this project. Let's stay late tonight and tomorrow and try to get back on track.

4. Let's _____ against Tim about this decision. It's clearly the wrong one for our company.

5. My kids always get _____ with games and never clean up!

6. Let's _____ your parents and see if they'll take us out for dinner tonight.

7. Let's _____ that wine you made. I think it's ready.

8. Cleaning the garage this weekend? I don't want to but let's _____.

9. Let's _____ our home security system. There have been a lot of break-ins recently.

Answers

1. stay within

2. end up

3. fall behind

4. fight back

5. carried away

6. hit up

7. break out

8. get it over with

9. beef up

Black and White

Terry and Sandra are Biology classmates discussing the issue of cloning.

Terry: What did you think about the **lecture** today? Interesting, right?

Sandra: The lecture raised a lot of ethical questions for me about **cloning**. It's not a **black and white** issue. There are so many **shades of gray**.

Terry: Definitely. There should be way stricter standards for replicating living things. At the end of the day, it shouldn't only come down to the researcher's **values** and **ethics**.

Sandra: Yes, **it goes without saying**. But who will **develop** these standards? Universities? **Industry**? The government?

Terry: That **remains to be seen**. Likely it'll be a combination of those things. Cloning is still a very new thing.

Vocabulary

lecture: In a university or college, where a professor gives information by talking about it. Typically, a 2-3 hour class that is held once a week.

cloning: Making a copy of something.

black and white: There *is* a clear right and wrong.

shades of gray: There *is no* clear right and wrong.

values: Basic, fundamental beliefs about something.

ethics: Moral principles that govern a person's behavior or the conducting of an activity.

it goes without saying: It's obvious.

develop: Make something new.

industry: For-profit companies.

remains to be seen: The outcome of something is undecided at the current time.

Practice

1. That _____ was so boring. I think I fell asleep for a few minutes.

2. That company has so many issues I think because they have no core _____.

3. It's a difficult situation! There are no _____ answers here.

4. Do you think that in 100 years from now, _____ of humans will be possible?

5. The university is putting together a committee to _____ some guidelines about cloning.

6. I can't tell you what to do in this situation. It depends on your personal _____.

7. You can make more money in _____ jobs than with the government but the benefits aren't as good.

8. It _____ whether or not I'll pass that test. It was so difficult.

9. _____ that he's the best choice for an advisor but he already has so many students.

10. I enjoy studying bioethics but I don't like that are so many _____ for almost everything.

Answers

1. lecture
2. values
3. black and white
4. cloning
5. develop
6. ethics/values
7. industry
8. remains to be seen
9. it goes without saying
10. shades of gray

Speak of the Devil

Jerry and Linda are talking about a guy that they both know.

Jerry: Have you seen Kenny lately? He **looks like a million bucks,** always wearing **flashy** clothes and driving his fancy new car.

Linda: I haven't seen him lately but guys like that are **a dime a dozen in this town.** They all made their money in finance, I think.

Jerry: **Speak of the devil!** I think I see him coming in the door right now! Let's call him over.

Linda: I don't want to **beat around the bush** so I'll just say it. I don't like Kenny! He **ripped me off** on his old TV that he sold me. It was hanging on by its' **last legs**.

Jerry: Let's **get out of here** then before he sees us.

Vocabulary

speak of the devil: The person you are talking about appears at that exact moment. For example, you are talking about a coworker and then they walk into the room right then.

looks like a million bucks: To look attractive or well put together.

a dime a dozen: Something that is very common, not special.

beat around the bush: Avoid talking about something important, or not getting to the main point directly.

ripped me off: To make a bad deal with someone. To be stolen from.

get out of here: To leave a place, usually quickly.

flashy: Bright, shiny, expensive.

last legs: Something that is close to breaking/stopping/not working.

Practice

1. Tim _____ these days with his new haircut.

2. Job offers like that are _____.

3. I want to _____ so badly! I hate this school.

4. "Oh, _____! We were just talking about you!"

5. Honestly, I hate that my boss loves to _____. I wish he'd just get to the point.

6. I'm so embarrassed that he_____.

7. My brother got a _____ new haircut in preparation for his job interview.

8. I'm going to have to buy a new car. This one is on its' _____.

Answers

1. looks like a million bucks

2. a dime a dozen

3. get out of here

4. speak of the devil

5. beat around the bush

6. ripped me off

7. flashy

8. last legs

Idioms #1

Ahead of the pack

Other forms: Front of the pack. In front of the pack.

Meaning: Used to describe who is in the lead or front of a group (often used for describing who is in the lead of a race or competition). To be ahead of other people or companies trying to do a similar thing. It's often used in business for a company that releases a certain product or technology before other companies.

Origin: "Pack" has been used to refer to a group of people since the 1400s. Or, it could be a reference to pack animals like dogs that have a leader that goes near the front.

Examples:

I think we can get ahead of the pack here and gain some serious market share.

There's no point in getting too far ahead of the pack. We'd have to wait for everyone else to catch up to us.

Get in front of the pack and don't look behind you. You'll never stay in the lead if you keep looking behind you.

Extra practice:

Think of a company that is ahead of the pack with a new product they have.

A lot on my plate

Other forms: She's/he's got a lot on her/his plate. I've got a lot on my plate. They've got a lot on their plates. We've got a lot on our plates.

Meaning: Many responsibilities. Used in a negative sense to imply that it's very difficult to manage everything. It can be used as a way to say, "no" to something. For example, "Sorry, I can't help out with that fundraiser. I've already got a lot on my plate."

Origin: First used in the 1900s. Refers to a plate that's heaping full of food and difficult to balance when carrying it to a table. Now, imagine those are your responsibilities!

Examples:

I have a lot on my plate with work and school. Final exams are coming soon.

She has a lot on her plate at work these days. She's managing three projects.

We've got a lot on our plate with the new baby and we both have demanding jobs.

Extra practice:

Think of a person you know who has a lot on their plate. What are they "juggling?"

Can't make heads or tails of it

Other forms: None.

Meaning: Unable to understand something. Can describe a work or school assignment, or someone's speech or behaviour.

Origin: Probably goes back to Ancient Rome. Cicero used a phrase that meant neither head nor feet to refer to confusion.

Examples:

What's he saying? I can't make heads or tails of it.

What do we have to do? I can't make heads or tails of this assignment.

Do you understand this spreadsheet? I can't make heads or tails of it.

Extra practice:

Think of a time when you couldn't make head or tails or something. What was it?

Break out in a cold sweat

Other forms: Breaks/broke/breaking out in a cold sweat (depends on the grammar in the sentence).

Meaning: To be terrified or very nervous about something.

Origin: Unknown but first seen around the 1500s. When some people get nervous, they sweat but also feel cold.

Examples:

I broke out in a cold sweat even thinking about that possibility.

My son breaks out in a cold sweat before tests. Once he starts, he's fine but he's so nervous before it.

I'm famous for breaking out in a cold sweat before I go on stage. I feel like I'm going to throw up.

Extra practice:

Think about a time when you broke out in a cold sweat. Why were you so scared or nervous?

Can't put my finger on it

Other forms: Can't quite put my finger on it.

Meaning: Unable to explain or totally comprehend something. Not sure exactly what is wrong.

Origin: From the 1800s. Refers to looking through a document and putting your finger onto something to support what you're looking for. If you can't find what you're looking for, then you can't put your finger on it.

Examples:

Something isn't right between Jenny and me but I can't put my finger on it.

I can't quite put my finger on it. Do you know what's up with Tommy?

Extra practice:

Think about a confusing situation you've experienced. Was their something about it that you couldn't put your finger on?

Back to square one

Other forms: None.

Meaning: Starting at the beginning again without progress or results.

Origin: It came from the days when people listened to soccer on the radio. Square one refers to the goal area. The commentator would often say back to square one because of all the passes back to the goaltender and free kicks when the ball goes out of bounds. It was often said with frustration because it's boring to just pass the ball back to the goaltender instead of going on the offensive.

Examples:

Well, we're back to square one on that project. Tim rejected our first attempt.

I'm back to square one on my thesis proposal. My advisor recommended against what I had in mind.

That project I was working on didn't get approved for funding.

Extra practice:

Think about a time when you had to go back to square one on an assignment or project.

My hands are tied

Other forms: His/her/our/their hands are tied.

Meaning: Used to explain not being able or permitted to do something because an authority/rule/law/situation/person won't allow it. Unable to do something, even if you wanted to.

Origin: First seen in the 1600s. Refers to being unable to do something because someone else has tied your hands together.

Examples:

Sorry, my hands are tied. I can't reverse that decision Johnny made.

I'd love to help you but my hands are tied.

Our hands are tied. We don't have access to the computer system to process a refund for that product.

Extra practice:

Have you ever been in a situation where your hands were tied and you were unable to do anything?

Chill Out

Keith is telling Sam that he's going to leave.

Keith: Hey, I think I'm going to **bail**.

Sam: **Chill out**! You just got here. Why are you leaving?

Keith: I'm tired of playing **third wheel** with you **couch potatoes**.

Sam: Come on, stay. We'll watch **a flick** or something.

Keith: Nah, I'm going to **roll**. I want to **catch some rays** at the beach.

Sam: You're such **a pain in the neck**! Why don't we come with you though? I'm tired of sitting around too.

Vocabulary

bail: Leave; depart.

chill out: Relax.

third wheel: Describes someone who is spending time with a couple.

couch potatoes: People who aren't that active, instead preferring to sit on the couch and watch TV or play video games.

a flick: A movie.

roll: Go somewhere.

catch some rays: Go outside in the sun.

a pain in the neck: Describes someone who is annoying or bothersome.

Practice

1. My youngest is such _____.

2. Let's _____. There are some weird people here.

3. I don't mind being the _____, depending on the couple.

4. Let's _____. We need to be there in 15 minutes.

5. I want to _____ this weekend for sure.

6. Hey, _____. We don't have to be there for another hour.

7. Do you want to catch _____ this weekend?

8. My kids are basically _____ and never want to go outside.

Answers

1. a pain in the neck

2. bail

3. third wheel

4. roll

5. catch some rays

6. chill out

7. a flick

8. couch potatoes

Talking About Bad Results

Brad and Jeremiah are talking about a problem with an advertising campaign.

Brad: I think we **missed the mark** on this radio advertising campaign.

Jeremiah: It's clear that there's no **one size fits all** solution. We have to **tailor** the ads to each radio station to account for demographic differences. We should have **pulled the plug** on it earlier too.

Brad: Maybe we did **jump the gun** on releasing them. I know we were in a **time crunch** at the end there.

Jeremiah: I **dropped the ball** on that one. We should have started working on them sooner.

Brad: We were way too **under the gun.** I'm not going to **take it lying down** though. Let's **regroup** and make those changes for the next round.

Vocabulary

missed the mark: Didn't achieve a hoped for result.

one size fits all: Something that is used for all instances or applications.

tailor: Adapt, change or modify.

pulled the plug: Stopped or finished something.

jump the gun: Started too early.

time crunch: Time pressure.

dropped the ball: Didn't do a good job.

under the gun: Feeling pressure.

take it lying down: Accept an insult or setback without complaint or protest.

regroup: To get organized and try again.

Practice

1. I don't want this to hold us back. Let's _____ and get back to it.

2. I'm happy he _____. We weren't getting anywhere with that group of people.

3. It's wishful thinking to believe that there's a _____ solution.

4. We need to fire him but I don't think he's going to _____.

5. We need to get moving on this or we're going to have a serious _____.

6. I'm nervous that we're going to _____ here. Let's take our time.

7. Ted is _____ on this project. He may have to do an all-nighter.

8. We need to _____ our offerings to each market segment.

9. I think Ted _____ on this one. He wasn't organized enough.

10. I may have _____. Let's go back to the drawing board.

Answers

1. regroup

2. pulled the plug

3. one size fits all

4. take it lying down

5. time crunch

6. jump the gun

7. under the gun

8. tailor

9. dropped the ball

10. missed the mark

Comprehension Questions

1. According to Brad, what is his assessment of the radio advertising campaign?
2. What does Jeremiah believe is the key issue with the advertising campaign, and what solution does he propose?
3. Why does Brad think they may have released the radio ads prematurely?
4. In Jeremiah's opinion, what mistake did he acknowledge making in relation to the advertising campaign?
5. How does Brad describe the time pressure they were under during the campaign's development?
6. Despite the challenges, what is Brad's attitude towards addressing the issues with the advertising campaign?
7. Based on the dialogue, what role does demographic targeting play in their evaluation of the advertising campaign's effectiveness?
8. In hindsight, what action does Jeremiah think they should have taken earlier in regards to the campaign?
9. How would you describe the overall tone of the conversation between Brad and Jeremiah regarding the advertising campaign?

Answers

1. According to Brad, his assessment of the radio advertising campaign is that they missed the mark.
2. Jeremiah believes the key issue with the advertising campaign is the lack of a one-size-fits-all solution. He proposes tailoring the ads to each radio station to account for demographic differences.
3. Brad thinks they may have released the radio ads prematurely because they were in a time crunch at the end.
4. Jeremiah acknowledges that he dropped the ball on not starting to work on the ads sooner.
5. Brad describes the time pressure they were under during the campaign's

development as being "in a time crunch at the end."

6. Despite the challenges, Brad's attitude towards addressing the issues with the advertising campaign is proactive. He suggests regrouping and making changes for the next round.

7. Demographic targeting is implied in Jeremiah's suggestion to tailor the ads to each radio station to account for demographic differences.

8. In hindsight, Jeremiah thinks they should have pulled the plug on the advertising campaign earlier.

9. The overall tone of the conversation between Brad and Jeremiah regarding the advertising campaign is reflective and focused on addressing the issues for improvement.

Discussion Questions

1. How crucial is demographic targeting in advertising campaigns, and what are some effective strategies for tailoring messages to different audiences?

2. In project management, how can teams strike a balance between the need for timely execution and the importance of thorough planning, particularly in time-sensitive projects?

3. How does tailoring content to specific channels or platforms contribute to the success of marketing and advertising initiatives? Can you provide examples from your own experience?

4. In time-sensitive projects, what strategies can teams employ to manage and cope with tight deadlines or being "under the gun"?

5. When a project faces setbacks, what steps can teams take to regroup, learn from the experience, and improve for future iterations?

Cover Up

Lindsay and Keith are talking about a political scandal.

Lindsay: Did you hear about that **cover up**? The prime minister got caught red-handed, finally.

Keith: I did. It was all over the news. At least he didn't **get away with** it this time. He also had to **hand over** all his tax records for the past 10 years.

Lindsay: The worst thing is that he kept **pointing to** his ex-wife, blaming her for all of this. I can't believe he **sustained** that scam for so many years.

Keith: He **screwed up**, big-time. I won't **put it past** me, that's for sure. I'm never voting for him again.

Lindsay: It's time to **stand for** something!

Vocabulary

cover up: Hide something.

get away with: Not get in trouble for bad behaviour.

hand over: Give something to someone.

pointing to: Blaming.

sustained: Kept going.

screwed up: Did something wrong.

put it past: Forget.

stand for: Have principles.

Practice

1. I think there's a _____ here somewhere. It's all so suspicious.

2. Please _____ the keys at 2:00 on Sunday.

3. Let's _____ us and try to move on.

4. Does he honestly _____ nothing? I don't trust him one bit.

5. My whole team is _____ each other, but in reality, it was Ted's fault that we lost the game.

6. The economy _____ the same growth rate this year as last.

7. She shouldn't be able to _____ stuff like that. What's her boss doing?

8. I have many faults, but I can always admit when I _____.

Answers

1. cover up

2. hand over

3. put it past

4. stand for

5. pointing to

6. sustained

7. get away with

8. screwed up

Vanished Into Thin Air

Amy and Chloe are talking about some criminal activity in their city.

Amy: Do you remember the story of that 2-year old boy who **vanished** into thin air?

Chloe: It was all over the news. I heard that he showed up at his mom's house in the middle of the night after 2 weeks, apparently **unscathed**.

Amy: It was the strangest thing. I heard that the police barely **investigated** it. They just assumed his dad took him. But there was no **evidence** of that at all.

Chloe: The investigation did seem rather **haphazard**.

Amy: They are pretty much **negligent**. Thankfully he's okay. I think we need to **reinforce** our policing system with some more officers.

Chloe: I'm not sure that's the answer. I think we need to **reform** the policing system and get rid of the **corrupt** people at the top.

Vocabulary

vanished: Disappeared quickly.

unscathed: Unharmed.

investigated: Looked into; examined.

evidence: Facts or information to prove or disprove something.

haphazard: Not carefully; lacking planning.

negligent: Lazy; neglectful.

reinforce: Make something stronger.

reform: Makes changes to improve a situation.

corrupt: A willingness to act dishonestly.

Practice

1. My keys seem to have _____. Will you help me look for them?

2. We need to _____ the management structure of our company.

3. I'm taking my doctor to court. I think he was _____.

4. You can go to war with your boss, but you won't escape _____.

5. Clean your room, but not in the _____ way you usually do it.

6. We need to _____ this fence, or it'll fall down.

7. I've _____ the matter, and I don't think Cindy did anything wrong.

8. Don't you think that all politicians are basically _____?

9. There's no _____ that she's been treating you unfairly. A feeling isn't enough.

Answers

1. vanished

2. reform

3. negligent

4. unscathed

5. haphazard

6. reinforce

7. investigated

8. corrupt

9. evidence

Greenhouse Gas Emissions

Sid and Drew are environmental science students who are discussing an issue.

Sid: Hey Drew. Did you hear that **greenhouse gas emissions** have gone way down since Covid started?

Drew: Oh yeah. I heard that. That's good news but I'm not sure it's enough to combat **rising sea levels** and the **melting ice caps** due to decades of overconsumption and pollution. Not to mention all the holes in the **ozone layer**. **In the long run**, it won't make much difference.

Sid: Oh, I hear you. We need to develop more **clean energy** sources. The old **reduce, reuse and recycle** thing isn't good enough. We need **systemic change**.

Drew: I **totally agree** with you. Global warming will lead to humanity's **ultimate** demise.

Vocabulary

greenhouse gas emissions: What is released (mainly carbon dioxide) when fossil fuels are burned.

rising sea levels: How the level of the ocean is increasing year after year.

melting ice caps: There is less ice at the North and South poles because they are melting due to climate change.

in the long run: Over a long period of time.

ozone layer: A layer in the atmosphere that absorbs the UV rays from the sun.

clean energy: Renewable energy like wind, water, and sun.

reduce, reuse, recycle: A slogan about what people can do to help the environment.

systemic change: Change that happens from the top, usually at the government level.

totally agree: Complete agreement about something.

ultimate: The last or final thing.

Practice

1. We need to do more as a country to reduce _____.

2. We can each do our part to save the environment but _____ is also important.

3. Some people will have to leave their island homes in the next few years because of _____.

4. We can all do more to _____.

5. I _____ with you about this! You don't have to convince me.

6. The holes in the _____ are getting bigger and bigger each year.

7. The _____ downfall of our world will be water scarcity.

8. Polar bears are having a difficult time because of the _____.

9. Changing to an electric car will save money _____.

10. Wind and solar power are examples of _____.

Answers

1. greenhouse gas emissions

2. systemic change

3. rising sea levels

4. reduce, reuse, and recycle

5. totally agree

6. ozone layer

7. ultimate

8. melting ice caps

9. in the long run

10. clean energy

Core Values

Lindsey and Ted are talking about a partnership with Tim, a business associate.

Lindsey: I'd like to talk to you about something.

Ted: Sure, what's up?

Lindsey: I'm **not comfortable with** our partnership with Tim anymore. I know it's **highly profitable** but I don't want to be **associated with** him. It raises questions about what our **core values** are.

Ted: I agree. I think we should **take action** on this **as soon as possible**. I've been having the same doubts. We're not quite **breaking the law** but what we're doing isn't really above board.

Lindsey: Okay, good. I'm happy that we're **on the same page**.

Vocabulary

not comfortable with: Not feeling relaxed about something.

highly profitable: Something that can make a lot of money.

associated with: Connected to.

core values: A person or an organization's most important beliefs.

take action: Do something.

as soon as possible: Quickly, at the first possible opportunity.

breaking the law: Doing something illegal.

on the same page: Agree about something.

Practice

1. I'm _____ going out alone at night.

2. One of our _____ is to care for the environment.

3. I want to finish up this assignment _____.

4. My husband and I are _____ with our budget.

5. Even though it's _____, it takes up too much of my time to continue with it.

6. Let's _____ on this tomorrow morning.

7. I can't believe that jaywalking is considered _____ in this city.

8. I don't want to be _____ that guy. Nothing good will come of it.

Answers

1. not comfortable with

2. core values

3. as soon as possible

4. on the same page

5. highly profitable

6. take action

7. breaking the law

8. associated with

When Pigs Fly

Jerry and Linda are talking about their kids.

Jerry: My kids are **buttering me up** because they don't want to have to help put up **Christmas lights.**

Linda: You're lucky that you can get some help **once in a while**. My kids never **pitch in** for stuff like that. **When pigs fly**, right?

Jerry: Ah, it's all **smoke and mirrors** at my house usually. My kids **make a show out of** cleaning up after themselves after dinner but their rooms are still like a **pigsty**.

Linda: What have we gotten ourselves into?

Vocabulary

when pigs fly: Something that is very unlikely to happen.

pitch in: To contribute to or help with something.

buttering me up: To flatter or please someone because you want something in return. For example, a child who is extra nice to their parents around Christmas because they want an expensive video game system.

smoke and mirrors: Flashy things that distract from what is real.

Christmas lights: Lights on houses for decoration around Christmas.

once in a while: Sometimes.

make a show out of: To do something in a flashy way.

pigsty: Usually refers to a very messy room or space.

Practice

1. I like to let loose _____.

2. His presentation was all _____. No real substance.

3. My kids love to help me put up _____.

4. We all _____ every Saturday morning to clean up the house.

5. My kid's bedroom is a _____.

6. My mom always used to say, "_____" when I asked her for money!

7. I know when my kids are _____ but I fall for it anyway. Their sweet smiles!

8. I hate that my coworkers always _____ finishing even the smallest task.

Answers

1. once in a while

2. smoke and mirrors

3. Christmas lights

4. pitch in

5. pigsty

6. When pigs fly

7. buttering me up

8. make a show out of

Asking for Clarification

Harper is asking for clarification from Logan.

Harper: Just so I'm clear on this: you're asking me to **scale back** production on Model 1234?

Logan: Yes, correct. Fuel prices are **skyrocketing** and there isn't as much demand for things that aren't fuel-efficient. Put it on the **backburner** for now.

Harper: Is this the plan **for the long haul**?

Logan: **Pretty much** as long as fuel prices remain at current levels and we're **in the red**. We're **feeling the pinch** with our expansion into Canada and we just don't have **money to burn** like we did a few years ago.

Harper: Okay, I got it. I'll let my team know.

Vocabulary

scale back: Reduce something.

skyrocketing: Increasing rapidly

backburner: Leave something for now and deal with it later.

for the long haul: For the long term.

pretty much: Almost 100% certain.

in the red: Losing money.

feeling the pinch: Experiencing financial difficulties.

money to burn: Extra money to spend freely.

Practice

1. Look at that new car he bought. He must have _____.

2. My company is in it _____.

3. I'm worried about this project that's now running _____.

4. We're _____ with Covid-19.

5. I _____ only want to know where I stand with this company.

6. Let's put this on the _____ until the economy recovers.

7. Fuel prices are _____ these days with the shortages.

8. Let's _____ production until the new model comes out.

Answers

1. money to burn

2. for the long haul

3. in the red

4. feeling the pinch

5. pretty much

6. backburner

7. skyrocketing

8. scale back

Get Into Trouble

Ian is talking to Ted about his many problems on the weekend.

Ted: Hey Ian, how was your weekend?

Ian: Oh, I **got into trouble** again! I got a **parking ticket, got lost** while hiking and then maybe got **food poisoning**.

Ted: Oh wow. That sounds terrible. You always have interesting stories though, right?

Ian: I'm **envious of** your life. It seems much calmer.

Ted: Well, it's **not all rainbows and unicorns**. I **asked somebody out** but she rejected me. I'm thinking about **giving up** on dating altogether.

Ian: Hang in there my friend. There are **plenty of fish in the sea**.

Vocabulary

got into trouble: Had some problems happen.

parking ticket: A fine you have to pay for parking illegally.

got lost: Didn't know where you were.

food poisoning: Getting sick from something that you ate.

envious of: Jealous of.

not all rainbows and unicorns: Real life isn't as good as it appears to others.

asked somebody out: Asked someone if they wanted to go on a date.

giving up: Stop trying.

plenty of fish in the sea: There are many eligible people to date.

Practice

1. He _____ out hiking because he didn't have any extra clothes or food and then he got lost.

2. When was the last time you _____? Maybe that's why you don't have a girlfriend!

3. I _____ all the time when I was visiting Seoul. It's such a big city!

4. Do you think that maybe it's _____? Why don't you go to the ER?

5. I'm _____ Joe. He always seems to have so many ladies to go on dates with.

6. I'm thinking about _____ scuba diving. It's such an expensive hobby.

7. Things are not always as they appear. My life is _____.

8. I know you're sad but there are _____.

9. If you don't pay your _____ on time, the fine doubles after a month.

Answers

1. got into trouble

2. asked somebody out

3. got lost

4. food poisoning

5. envious of

6. giving up

7. not all rainbows and unicorns

8. plenty of fish in the sea

9. parking ticket

Noise Pollution

Kathleen and Kenny are talking about living in Busan.

Kathleen: Kenny! You lived in Busan, South Korea? I've always wanted to go there. What's it like? I've heard that it's a beautiful **coastal city**.

Kenny: Well, there's a lot of **noise pollution** and **light pollution**. It's the second biggest city in Korea. And **traffic jams** too during **rush hour**.

Kathleen: It sounds terrible.

Kenny: Oh no, it's amazing! I love Nampo-Dong, which has lots of **street food** and **street vendors** plus **trendy cafes**. It's perfect for a date.

Kathleen: What else?

Kenny: Well, there's no real **downtown core** or **main square** but there are six beaches within **city limits**. Most people just hang out there, especially in the summertime.

Vocabulary

coastal city: A city next to the ocean.

noise pollution: Ambient noise in a city. For example, cars honking.

light pollution: Light from signs and cars that you can see inside your house at night.

traffic jams: Lots of cars on the road which makes progress slower than normal.

rush hour: The busiest times to drive, usually because of people going to work and coming home from work.

street food: Food from an outside stall.

street vendors: People selling things at an outside stall.

trendy cafes: Coffee shops that are fashionable and hip.

downtown core: The area in a city with lots of tall buildings; an important place of business.

main square: The most important public courtyard in a city.

city limits: The outer edge of the city, including suburbs. Not just the downtown core.

Practice

1. I love to buy Christmas presents from _____. There are lots of interesting things.

2. Vancouver is the best _____ in Canada.

3. Within the _____, you can find three beaches and countless parks.

4. Go after 9:30 am to avoid ____.

5. Where's the _____? I'd love to spend some time there and people watch.

6. The best _____ in Korea? Honestly, I can't choose. There are many delicious things.

7. The _____ in Edmonton is famous for being boring at night.

8. ____ makes it difficult for me to sleep at night even though I have blackout curtains.

9. My boyfriend loves to spend time at _____ on weekends. I think they're expensive!

10. During ____, it takes twice as long to get home.

11. The _____ is terrible here. I have to wear earplugs to sleep at night.

Answers

1. street vendors

2. coastal city

3. city limits

4. traffic jams

5. main square

6. street food

7. downtown core

8. light pollution

9. trendy cafes

10. rush hour

11. noise pollution

Idioms #2

An apple a day keeps the doctor away

Other forms: None.

Meaning: Eating healthy keeps you from getting sick. Apple represents all healthy food in this idiom.

Origin: First seen in the late 1800s to early 1900s in Wales. In old English, an apple could refer to any round fruit so it may be related to the fact that healthy eating is vital for good health.

Examples:

My mother used to say, "An apple a day keeps the doctor away."

Don't forget that an apple a day keeps the doctor away! Stop eating so much junk food!

Eat lots of fruits and veggies if you want to live a long life. An apple a day keeps the doctor away.

Extra practice:

Do you agree, or disagree with this idiom? Can eating healthy food prevent illness?

Card up my sleeve

Other forms: None.

Meaning: A secret advantage to be used later.

Origin: From the 1800s. Refers to gamblers who hide a winning card in their shirtsleeve and then pull it out at the right time to win.

Examples:

Owen always has a card up his sleeve. He'll pull through in the end even though it seems like he won't finish the project on time.

I wish I had a card up my sleeve but all my chips are on the table now. This is all I have for a down payment for a house.

I hope you have a card up your sleeve. We need to do something or we'll lose the bid.

Extra practice:

Do you know anyone who always seems to have a card up their sleeve?

(As) busy as a beaver

Other forms: (As) busy as a bee.

Meaning: Working a lot or very hard.

Origin: Beavers are very hard workers who spend lots of time building dams and lodges. Same with bees who work very hard to make honey and build hives.

Examples:

You're as busy as a beaver these days with all your homework.

I'm as busy as a beaver with the holidays approaching.

You're busy as a bee these days with work and school! I never get to see you.

Extra practice:

Is there a period in your life when you've been as busy as a beaver? What were you doing at the time?

Cash in your chips

Other forms: None.

Meaning: Quit or stop doing something before possibly losing what you have won (or achieved), or before the situation gets worse so that the positives you have are not lost. Can also refer to dying—you are out of the game (life).

Origin: From the 1900s. Gamblers turn in their chips for the cash equivalent when they're finished playing.

Examples:

Don't you think it's time to cash in your chips and quit? That job is terrible.

Let's cash in our chips and be done with this company, okay?

Sometimes you just have to cash in your chips, you know? You've already wasted so much time on this project that's going nowhere.

Extra practice:

Have you ever been forced to cash in your chips on something? What happened?

Bite the bullet

Other forms: Bit/biting/bites the bullet (depends on the grammar in the sentence).

Meaning: Resolve to do something difficult that you've been procrastinating or hesitating on and just get it over with.

Origin: Unknown. But, one theory is that patients had to bite a bullet when undergoing surgery before anesthesia was developed to endure the pain. However, a leather strap was most often used for this purpose and not a bullet.

Examples:

Let's just bite the bullet and get this report done before we go home.

You're going to have to bite the bullet and apologize to her. She's not going to back down.

I know that biting the bullet isn't your style but you're going to need to buckle down and study if you want to pass this test.

Extra practice:

Have you ever had to bite the bullet and do something difficult that you were procrastinating or hesitating on and didn't really want to do? What was it?

At the eleventh hour

Other forms: Can be used with various prepositions instead of "at." For example: during, in, until, etc. See the examples below.

Meaning: At the very last minute.

Origin: Possibly from Mathew 20:9 in the Bible. In this story, each worker received a denarius (unit of currency) for a day of work, even those who started at hour 11 in a 12-hour day.

Examples:

That meeting got called at the eleventh hour, right before I was getting ready to leave.

The two parties finally came to an agreement during the eleventh hour negotiations.

Extra practice:

Have you ever had something happen at the eleventh hour? Why did it happen so late?

Talking about a Customer

Emma is talking to Oliver about one of their customers.

Emma: Hey, so I was just talking to Noah and it looks like they won't renew the contract. It's a bit **up in the air** but I think they want to **sever ties** with us.

Oliver: To me, **the writing is on the wall**. They haven't been happy for months now.

Emma: Not to **throw someone under the bus** but the **elephant in the room** is Mia's performance as their account manager. It's just not good enough.

Oliver: I think you've **hit the nail on the head**. She's already **in the dog house** with that other account she manages.

Emma: She's **all talk**. It's time she **puts her money where her mouth is**.

Oliver: I'd love to go behind her back and **blow the whistle** on this but I don't want to draw attention to myself.

Vocabulary

up in the air: Not decided yet.

sever ties: To stop a relationship.

the writing is on the wall: It's obvious to everyone.

throw someone under the bus: To blame someone for something.

the elephant in the room: The obvious thing that nobody is talking about.

hit the nail on the head: See the problem clearly.

in the dog house: In trouble.

all talk: Good at talking but their actions don't reflect this.

puts her money where her mouth is: Her actions need to reflect her words.

blow the whistle: To disclose true information that might be harmful to someone.

Practice

1. Honestly, I just think he should _____ on his company. They're doing some terrible things.

2. I'm _____ with my kids if I get home too late from work.

3. I think we need to _____ with that contractor.

4. Why is nobody talking about _____?

5. It's time for her to _____ and do some work.

6. He's _____ but no action.

7. I hate that we have to _____ for this.

8. You've made a good point and _____ exactly.

9. Don't you think that _____? I'm going to get fired.

10. I don't think she's made the decision yet. It's still _____.

Answers

1. blow the whistle

2. in the dog house

3. sever ties

4. the elephant in the room

5. put her money where her mouth is

6. all talk

7. throw someone under the bus

8. hit the nail on the head

9. the writing is on the wall

10. up in the air

Vanished Into Thin Air

Amy and Chloe are talking about some criminal activity in their city.

Amy: Do you remember the story of that 2-year old boy who **vanished** into thin air?

Chloe: It was all over the news. I heard that he showed up at his mom's house in the middle of the night after 2 weeks, apparently **unscathed**.

Amy: It was the strangest thing. I heard that the police barely **investigated** it. They just assumed his dad took him. But there was no **evidence** of that at all.

Chloe: The investigation did seem rather **haphazard**.

Amy: They are pretty much **negligent**. Thankfully he's okay. I think we need to **reinforce** our policing system with some more officers.

Chloe: I'm not sure that's the answer. I think we need to **reform** the policing system and get rid of the **corrupt** people at the top.

Vocabulary

vanished: Disappeared quickly.

unscathed: Unharmed.

investigated: Looked into; examined.

evidence: Facts or information to prove or disprove something.

haphazard: Not carefully; lacking planning.

negligent: Lazy; neglectful.

reinforce: Make something stronger.

reform: Makes changes to improve a situation.

corrupt: A willingness to act dishonestly.

Practice

1. My keys seem to have _____. Will you help me look for them?

2. We need to _____ the management structure of our company.

3. I'm taking my doctor to court. I think he was _____.

4. You can go to war with your boss, but you won't escape _____.

5. Clean your room, but not in the _____ way you usually do it.

6. We need to _____ this fence, or it'll fall down.

7. I've _____ the matter, and I don't think Cindy did anything wrong.

8. Don't you think that all politicians are basically _____?

9. There's no _____ that she's been treating you unfairly. A feeling isn't enough.

Answers

1. vanished

2. reform

3. negligent

4. unscathed

5. haphazard

6. reinforce

7. investigated

8. corrupt

9. evidence

Knowledge-Based Economy

A TA is discussing an issue in an Economics tutorial.

Canada is now a **knowledge-based economy**. Workers who ignore that do so at their own **peril**. Most of the **manufacturing** jobs, and especially the good **union** jobs, have now been **outsourced** to places with cheaper labour like India or China. Those who lack the skills to operate in a digital world risk being left out of the **job market** altogether.

One option is **retraining**. However, that can be quite difficult with older workers who are not that familiar with using computers. It can be an **uphill battle**. There are some **alternatives** as well as to what to do for these workers who get **laid off** from manufacturing jobs. Has anyone seen any approaches mentioned in the news lately? Let's talk about some of the new programs.

Vocabulary

knowledge-based economy: A kind of economy where information or intellectual skills are most important.

peril: Risk.

manufacturing: Making something.

union: An organization that negotiates for and protects a group of workers from employers.

outsourced: Work that is sent to another country, company, etc.

job market: Where employees look for jobs and employers look for workers.

retraining: Learning new skills for a different kind of job than currently doing.

uphill battle: Describes something very difficult to do or achieve.

alternatives: Other options.

laid off: A worker is temporarily or permanently stopped from working because of a situation out of their control.

Practice

1. Older people often have a difficult time adapting to a _____.

2. The _____ is great for employees these days. Wages keep going up.

3. Good _____ jobs with benefits are difficult to find in Europe these days.

4. Learning computer skills later in life is an _____ for some people.

5. My company _____ customer service to India last year.

6. We'll have to switch to digital records soon. If we don't, it's at our own ____.

7. My wife got _____ when her company went out of business.

8. I might do some _____ and learn how to become a car mechanic.

9. Why don't you consider the _____ before making a decision? You're overlooking some of them.

10. The _____ dues (fees) are quite high but it's maybe worth it? The union did negotiate a good contract for us last year.

Answers

1. knowledge-based economy

2. job market

3. manufacturing

4. uphill battle

5. outsourced

6. peril

7. laid off

8. retraining

9. alternatives

10. union

Confusing Words: Accept/Except

Listening/pronunciation tip: These two words only have a slight difference in pronunciation which makes them confusing. Focus on the first vowel sound of each word. "Accept" has a sharp and short "a" like in "apple," whereas the first sound of "except" has an "e" like in "egg."

accept: A verb that means to take or receive something (willingly, with permission). It can also mean to believe or recognize an opinion, story, or theory.

Most people accept that the theory of evolution is true.

I accepted the job offer. I'll start in two weeks.

His parents accepted his decision to not go to college.

I can't accept his apology. What he did was just so bad.

except: Used as a preposition to mean not including or other than; not included, something not a part of a grouping. Also used as a verb but not commonly (usually in legal documents).

That restaurant is open every day except for Mondays.

The letter is great except for one thing—there are a few spelling mistakes. Use spell check on your computer.

He does nothing except complain. I'm so tired of it.

I have to work every day except for Tuesdays.

Practice

1. Are you going to _____ the revised contract?

2. That house is good, _____ it only has one bathroom.

3. We're open for lunch, _____ on Tuesdays.

4. Can you _____ my package for me, please? It's going to be delivered on my day off.

5. Please _____ my sincere apology.

6. He's a great employee _____ he always shows up a few minutes late.

Answers

1. accept

2. except

3. except

4. accept

5. accept

6. except

Speaking practice: After checking your fill-in-the-blank answers, try speaking each sentence to a friend. Or, record yourself speaking each sentence on your smartphone. Then listen and see if your pronunciation is clear and easy to understand.

Feeling Under the Weather

Jerry is talking to his friend Linda about being sick.

Jerry: I know, I know. My mom used to tell me to not be such a **couch potato** and that **an apple a day keeps the doctor away**. I wish that I'd listened to her! I'm feeling **worse for wear.**

Linda: Keep your chin up! I know you're **feeling under the weather** but **this too shall pass.**

Jerry: Thanks Linda, I appreciate you **checking in on** me every day.

Linda: It's the least I can do. You've helped me with so many things over the years. Just don't **kick the bucket** on me, okay?

Vocabulary

feeling under the weather: Not feeling well; feeling sick.

keep your chin up: Telling something to stay strong. Encouraging someone in a tough situation.

couch potato: Someone who spends lots of time on the couch watching TV or movies or playing video games. Not active.

an apple a day keeps the doctor away: Eating healthy keeps you from getting sick.

this too shall pass: A bad period of time that will eventually end.

checking in on: To see how someone is doing.

it's the least I can do: No problem; it's a small thing, usually when you feel like you should do more.

worse for wear: Feeling worn out or tired.

kick the bucket: Die.

Practice

1. My dad keeps phoning and _____ me. It's almost too much!

2. I keep nagging my son to get active because he's such a _____.

3. I called in sick because I was feeling a bit _____.

4. My mom is great at telling people to _____ when something bad happens.

5. I'm convinced that the saying, "_____" really does work!

6. My son has been pretty down lately but I told him that, "_____."

7. Lunch is on me. _____, seeing as you've been making me meals all week.

8. I'm _____ after being in the hospital for more than a week. It was impossible to sleep there.

9. I hope that I don't _____ before I'm 80 but I'm nervous about how much I smoke!

Answers

1. checking in on

2. couch potato

3. under the weather

4. keep your chin up

5. An apple a day keeps the doctor away

6. This too shall pass

7. It's the least I can do

8. worse for wear

9. kick the bucket

Break Up

Keith is talking to Carrie about breaking up with her boyfriend.

Carrie: Did you **break up** with Chris yet?

Keith: I was hoping you wouldn't ask me that question! I can't **go through with** it. I'm worried that he's going to be **pissed off** at me.

Carrie: You can **let him off** easily though, right? Be super kind. I know that you don't like **hanging around** with him.

Keith: It's true, yes. I need to **shake things up** and finally end it. Let me go do it right now before I **talk myself out of** it.

Vocabulary

break up: End a romantic relationship.

go through with: Do something that you have planned in advance.

pissed off: Be angry at someone or about something.

let him off: Release.

hanging around: Spending time with.

shake things up: Make a change.

talk myself out of: Convince yourself not to do something.

Practice

1. I think you should _____ with Tony. He's not a good guy!

2. Jay is _____ because I made him clean his room.

3. I have to not _____ asking women out. I just get so nervous

4. Sid and Jen are _____ together a lot these days. Maybe they'll start dating?

5. I'm not sure I can _____ the tattoo. It seems so painful.

6. We need to _____ a bit. Maybe we need to fire one of the low-performers?

7. I'm not sure you should _____ so easily. He needs some punishment for what he did. You don't always need to be the good guy.

Answers

1. break up

2. pissed off

3. talk myself out of

4. hanging around

5. go through with

6. shake things up

7. let him off

Nice Weather and Weekend Plans

Tim and Carrie are talking about their weekend plans.

Tim: The weather looks great for the weekend. Do you have any plans?

Carrie: I'm going to get my garden ready for planting. I have **my work cut out for me**. It's so overgrown. But, it's not **set in stone**. I'll see what else comes up!

Tim: Yeah, it is that time of year, right? The days are getting longer. I'm going to **play it by ear**. Honestly, I'm pretty **burned out** and am **barely treading water**. The **fallout** from the **cost-cutting measures** has had a huge impact on me.

Carrie: Sorry to hear that. Is there anything I can do to help?

Tim: Nah, it's okay. Gotta **bring home the bacon**, right? It's not all **doom and gloom**. I may go to a movie or something.

Carrie: You **got hit hard by** that. Don't you want to **throw in the towel?**

Vocabulary

my work cut out for me: A big or difficult job to do.

set in stone: Decided 100%.

burned out: Tired, stressed and overworked.

treading water: Barely keeping up with work or school.

fallout: Negative consequences.

cost-cutting measures: Something done to save money.

bring home the bacon: Make money with a job.

doom and gloom: Only bad things.

got hit hard by: To be badly affected by something.

throw in the towel: To quit or give up.

63

Practice

1. I'm barely _____ at my new job and am worried that I'll get fired.

2. We're not the only ones who _____ by Covid-19.

3. I hate my job but someone has to _____.

4. It's not all _____. He did get a B+ in English.

5. I have _____ with this new team.

6. I quit that job because I was so _____.

7. The _____ went too far I think. We're so understaffed now.

8. Nobody anticipated this would be the _____ from that decision.

9. Someone has to get fired but nothing is _____.

10. I'm ready to _____ on that project! It's brought me nothing but grief.

Answers

1. treading water

2. got hit hard by

3. bring home the bacon

4. doom and gloom

5. my work cut out for me

6. burned out

7. cost-cutting measures

8. fallout

9. set in stone

10. throw in the towel

Online Dating

Jen and Tina are talking about online dating.

Jen: Hey, so what's new with you **these days**?

Tina: Oh, not much. But I did start doing **online dating**.

Jen: Nice! How's that going?

Tina: It's like finding a **needle in a haystack**. I mean, they don't have to look like **movie stars** but I'm so tired of guys with **facial hair**—**shaggy beards** and **bushy eyebrows**. Gross.

Jen: So what are you looking for?

Tina: Nothing complicated. Someone with an **athletic build**, **outgoing personality**, and a **good sense of humour**. Shouldn't be too difficult, right?

Vocabulary

these days: Lately; recently.

online dating: Finding a love match through the Internet.

needle in a haystack: Describes something that is difficult to find.

movie stars: Famous actors or actresses.

facial hair: Beard or mustache.

shaggy beards: Beards that are not well-groomed.

bushy eyebrows: Big eyebrows that are not well-groomed.

athletic build: Describes someone in good shape who exercises a lot.

outgoing personality: Describes someone who likes being around people.

good sense of humor: Describes someone who likes to laugh and tell jokes.

Practice

1. What have you been up to _____?

2. How did he get such an _____? He must be working out a lot.

3. Guys with _____ are all the rage lately.

4. Finding my keys in the morning is like finding a _____.

5. I love that my co-worker has such a _____. I'm always laughing.

6. Who are your favourite _____?

7. I'm thinking about growing out my _____. What do you think?

8. I hate my _____. It's so much work to keep them trimmed.

9. I'm looking for someone with an _____ because I'm kind of shy.

10. I know that you don't want to but I think you'd have good luck with _____.

Answers

1. these days

2. athletic build

3. shaggy beards

4. needle in a haystack

5. good sense of humour

6. movie stars

7. facial hair

8. bushy eyebrows

9. outgoing personality

10. online dating

Come Apart

Bob: Hey, how are you doing these days? Didn't you just have your third child?

Kent: I sometimes feel like I **can't go on**. I'm starting to **come apart** at the seams. I have to work all the time to **pay for** everything and my wife just **went back** to work too. We have no time to do anything fun.

Bob: That sounds tough. I remember when you used to **come out** for beers with the boys! Those days are done for a while I guess.

Kent: I'd love to **get back to** that one day. Maybe not for a while though.

Bob: Hang in there my friend! **Cheer up**!

Vocabulary

can't go on: Too tired to continue.

come apart: Break down.

pay for: Spend money on something or someone.

went back: Returned.

come out: Leave the house to do something with people.

get back to: Return to doing something.

hang in there: Don't give up.

cheer up: Be happy!

Practice

1. I _____ with that job anymore. I hate it so much.

2. Having a drink with the boys is so fun until someone has to _____ it!

3. I _____ to school in my thirties to become a lawyer.

4. _____ with studying for your test. It's coming up soon.

5. Why don't you _____ with us tonight? We're going to grab a few drinks.

6. _____! It could have certainly been worse.

7. Let's _____ work.

8. The lining in your suit jacket is starting to _____. Why don't you replace it?

Answers

1. can't go on

2. pay for

3. went back

4. hang in there

5. come out

6. cheer up

7. get back to

8. come apart

Conned Out Of

Terry is talking to Lauren about how he lost some money.

Terry: So I just got **conned out of** $1000! This salesman guy on *Craigslist* tricked me into buying a TV that doesn't even work.

Lauren: **Hang on**. Did you report it to the police?

Terry: No. I feel embarrassed about it. I didn't want to **come forward**.

Lauren: **Come on**. It won't take long to **fill out** the form at the police station. They see this kind of thing all the time. I'll **go with** you. I hate seeing you get screwed out of that much cash.

Terry: You're right. Let's **get it over with**. Maybe I can get some justice.

Vocabulary

conned out of: Tricked; fooled.

hang on: Wait.

come forward: Report something.

come on: Encouragement to do something.

fill out: Write information on a form.

go with: Join together.

get it over with: Do something that you don't want to do.

Practice

1. My grandpa was _____ his life-savings.

2. You have to _____ and report that guy!

3. Taxes! Let's just _____ now.

4. Please _____ this form and we'll get back to you if we're interested.

5. _____ a second. This is important. What's that website URL again?

6. Why don't I _____ you? It won't be so bad then. We'll grab some *Starbucks* before we go too.

7. _____. Keep going! You're almost there.

Answers

1. conned out of

2. come forward

3. get it over with

4. fill out

5. hang on

6. go with

7. come on

Idioms #3

Bring a lot to the table

Other forms: Brought/brings/bringing a lot to the table

Meaning: Someone who provides things that can benefit a person, group, or place. For example, they have a lot of skills, experience, money, wisdom, talent, etc. Used most often to describe employees.

Origin: It could refer to the amount of money that a gambler brings to the table to play with. Or, social or religious feasts where everyone is expected to contribute something to the table.

Examples:

I think Julie brings a lot to the table. Why don't we hire her?

Jeremy doesn't bring much to the table. He should be the first guy we let go.

Tony brought a lot to the table during that last project. Shouldn't we give him a raise?

Extra practice:

Think of someone at work who brings a lot to the table. What skills do they possess?

Cool as a cucumber

Other forms: None.

Meaning: Very calm or relaxed in a stressful situation.

Origin: Unknown but cucumbers always feel cool and fresh inside, no matter how hot it is.

Examples:

My friend is an air traffic controller and is always as cool as a cucumber.

Cool as a cucumber? I'm the complete opposite of that—always stressed out.

You have to remain cool as a cucumber during the negotiations or they'll eat you alive.

Extra practice:

Think of a person that you know who is as cool as a cucumber.

Corner the market

Other forms: Cornered/corners/cornering the market (depends on the grammar in the sentence).

Meaning: Gain a lot of the market share in order to have an influential position to be able to manipulate prices. Always used in a business context.

Origin: Unknown, but likely originated in the 1800s with the beginning of the market economy.

Examples:

I'm hoping we can corner the market with our new release.

Apple cornered the market with their new phone.

We're doing a good job of cornering the market with that new release. Let's keep at it and double down on our marketing efforts.

Extra practice:

Think of a company who has cornered the market with one of their products.

Back to the drawing board

Other forms: None.

Meaning: To start over after making a failed attempt at something.

Origin: From cartoonist Peter Arno in The New Yorker in 1941. The cartoon has a burning airplane with the military pilot coming down by parachute. The civilian engineer has design plans under his arms and the caption says, "Well, back to the drawing board."

Examples:

It's back to the drawing board—the client didn't like the first schematics.

The government regulators rejected our modifications so it's back to the drawing board.

Let's get back to the drawing board. Tina didn't like our first draft.

Extra practice:

Think of a time when you had to go back to the drawing board. How did you feel when that happened?

Beat around the bush

Other forms: Beating around the bush (depends on the grammar in the sentence).

Meaning: Avoid talking about something important, or not getting to the main point directly. Some people do this unintentionally because they're not good communicators. Others do this because they're avoiding a difficult topic (for example, telling someone that they're fired).

Origin: From the early 1400s. Rich men used to hire people to beat the bushes when they went hunting to scare the birds out of them so that they could shoot them.

Examples:

Let's not beat around the bush—the blame lies with Logan for this problem. Nobody else.

I hate that my boss always beats around the bush which makes meetings take way longer than they need to.

Stop beating around the bush. Just tell me what you need me to do in this situation. I'm tired of trying to guess what you need.

Extra practice:

Think of someone you know who beats around the bush. How do you feel when talking to them?

Costs an arm and a leg

Other forms: Costing/cost an arm and a leg (depends on the grammar in the sentence).

Meaning: Very expensive; usually more than you can afford.

Origin: Uncertain but one theory is that it comes from painters in the 1700s. For portraits, the cheapest option was just the head and shoulders.

Examples:

Those couches cost an arm and a leg and I'm not sure they're worth it.

I saved up to buy a new Tesla, even though it costs an arm and a leg.

It's going to end up costing an arm and a leg to build a new deck. Is it worth it?

Extra practice:

Have you ever bought something that costs an arm and a leg? Was it worth it?

You can't Judge a Book by Its Cover

Jerry and Linda are talking about one of their new neighbors.

Jerry: Have you met our new neighbor yet?

Linda: I talked to him last night but he's **a hard nut to crack**. He only gave one-word answers to all my questions!

Jerry: Well, **you can't judge a book by its cover**. I'm sure we'll find out more about him as time goes on. Maybe he's not that **talkative.**

Linda: Maybe. But I felt frustrated talking to him for just a few minutes. Anyway, I'm working on not **burning bridges** so I'll **put my best foot forward**!

Jerry: Good plan. You never know **what may come**. Let's invite him over for dinner and see if he **opens up**.

Vocabulary

you can't judge a book by its cover: to not judge something or someone based on appearance. For example, a restaurant that's not stylish and new may have delicious food.

a hard nut to crack: Someone that is difficult to get to know.

burning bridges: Damaging relationships.

put my best foot forward: To be on one's best behaviour.

what may come: What could happen in the future.

talkative: Someone who likes to talk a lot.

opens up: Shares information about oneself.

Practice

1. I try my best to avoid _____ when leaving a job.

2. I'm happy for the fresh start and want to _____ at this new job.

3. My dad rarely talks and is _____.

4. I learned early on in life that _____.

5. I'm well prepared for _____.

6. My daughter is so _____. I go for a walk every day to get a break!

7. I love it when my son _____ to me. It happens so rarely!

Answers

1. burning bridges

2. put my best foot forward

3. a hard nut to crack

4. you can't judge a book by its cover

5. what may come

6. talkative

7. opens up

Talking About Strategy

Mason and Owen want to gain some market share.

Mason: I'm hoping that we can gain some **market share** on ABC company this year.

Owen: Them? They're **small fries** in my opinion. I'd love to gain the **upper hand** on XYX. I think it's **within our reach** if we can **ramp-up** production quickly enough.

Mason: To gain on them is a **long shot** for sure. But, it's potentially a **gold mine** if we become **top of mind** in that category instead of them.

Owen: Well, let's **give them a run for their money**. But, we can't forget about QRS. They're trying to **move in on** us.

Vocabulary

market share: A percentage of the overall market that a company holds.

small fries: Insignificant people or things.

upper hand: The controlling or dominant position.

within our reach: Can be obtained without too much difficulty.

ramp-up: To increase quickly.

long shot: Something that's unlikely to happen.

gold mine: Lucrative.

top of mind: The first thing people think of; the greatest priority or concern.

give them a run for their money: Provide good competition.

move in on: Get closer to a person or place. Usually to attack or take over.

Practice

1. It's time to _____ them. We've been waiting long enough!

2. I know it's a _____, but I'm hoping to make a million dollars in sales this year.

3. Let's _____. They're struggling right now and the timing is perfect for us.

4. Fuel efficiency should be _____ when buying a new car.

5. Coca-Cola and Pepsi are constantly fighting for more _____.

6. Let's _____ production on the black shoes. They're selling well.

7. I think the targets are _____ if we push hard this last quarter.

8. Developing software for businesses is potentially a _____.

9. I'm hoping to gain the _____ this year over my main competitor.

10. Those guys? I'm not worried. They're just _____.

Answers

1. move in on

2. long shot

3. give them a run for their money

4. top of mind

5. market share

6. ramp-up

7. within our reach

8. gold mine

9. upper hand

10. small fries

Comprehension Questions

1. What is Mason's goal for this year?
2. What does Owen suggest as a potential target for gaining market share, and why does he believe it's achievable?
3. What does Mason think about gaining market share from XYX?
4. According to Mason, what potential benefit could come from becoming "top of mind" in a particular category?
5. What does Owen mean when he says, "let's give them a run for their money"?
6. Who is trying to move in on the company, according to Owen, and why is it a concern?

Answers

1. Mason's goal for this year is to gain some market share, particularly from ABC company.
2. Owen suggests gaining the upper hand on XYX as a potential target for gaining market share. He believes it's achievable if they can ramp up production quickly.
3. Mason thinks gaining market share from XYX is a long shot but could be a potential gold mine if they become top of mind in that category.
4. According to Mason, the potential benefit of becoming "top of mind" in a category is that it could be a gold mine for the company.
5. When Owen says, "let's give them a run for their money," he means they should compete strongly with the competition.
6. According to Owen, QRS is trying to move in on the company, and it's a concern because they can't forget about QRS in their efforts to gain market share.

Discussion Questions

1. How do companies typically go about gaining market share in a competitive industry?

2. How might a company determine whether a competitor is considered a significant threat or "small fries" in the market?

3. When considering market share strategies, what role do production capacity and efficiency play in a company's success?

4. How important is it for a company to be "top of mind" in a specific category, and what benefits might come from achieving that status?

5. How might the overall economic climate and industry trends impact a company's ability to gain market share?

A Dilemma

Kevin and Tracy are talking about a situation at work.

Tracy: How are things going with your team?

Kevin: Not great. We keep missing deadlines and getting work sent back because it's not high enough quality. I don't know how to **mend** things. It's a real **dilemma**. As their **intrepid** leader, I feel like I've failed. I've tried to **evaluate** what's going on, but I'm not sure.

Tracy: Well, team **cohesion** is key. The **fundamental flaw** of your team seems to be a lack of team spirit. You need to be **cognizant** of the relationships between people.

Kevin: I'm terrible at that. That must be why we're struggling.

Tracy: Focus on creating a positive atmosphere. **Praise** goes a long way too!

Kevin: I'm happy that I talked to you about this.

Vocabulary

mend: To fix.

dilemma: A Situation requiring a difficult choice.

intrepid: Fearless.

evaluate: Assess.

cohesion: Uniting, or becoming one.

fundamental: Basic; of primary importance.

flaw: A feature that ruins the perfection of something.

cognizant: Being aware of something.

praise: To give approval or admiration.

Practice

1. Do you think we can _____ that zipper instead of throwing it out?

2. _____ is key to any team.

3. I have a _____. I said that I'd be in two places at the same time!

4. Please be _____ of that fact that I'm terribly out of shape! You'll have to walk a bit slower.

5. The _____ problem is that we have a hard time talking to each other.

6. Let's _____ what went wrong here.

7. A bit of _____ goes a long way! Tell people when they do a good job of something.

8. You're such an _____ traveler! I can't believe you did that by yourself.

9. It looks great. The only _____ is that you didn't cite your references in the correct format.

Answers

1. mend

2. cohesion

3. dilemma

4. cognizant

5. fundamental

6. evaluate

7. praise

8. intrepid

9. flaw

Complaining about a Co-worker

Jerry is telling Linda about a fight he had with a coworker.

Jerry: I just had a big fight with my friend and I'm not sure I can just **get over it.** It was a **massive blow-up**.

Linda: Oh no! What happened?

Jerry: Well, she's my co-worker and keeps **stealing my thunder** on work projects. She's taking credit for stuff that I do. I'm **sick and tired of it.** I just caught her **red-handed**.

Linda: That's a **tough pill to swallow**. I'd for sure have a **bee in my bonnet** about this too.

Jerry: It's not even **the straw that broke the camel's back.** She owes me a thousand **bucks** as well.

Linda: Honestly, she sounds like a **bad egg**.

Vocabulary

stealing my thunder: Taking credit for something that someone else did.

get over it: To fully recover (from an illness) or not think about it negatively anymore (break-up with a girlfriend or boyfriend, losing a job, etc.).

tough pill to swallow: Something difficult to get over.

bee in my bonnet: A certain issue that is annoying someone.

the straw that broke the camel's back: The last thing in a series of bad things before an event occurs — like a breakup, quitting a job, or fight.

blow-up: Big fight or problem.

massive: Very big/huge.

sick and tired of it: Annoyed by something that happens frequently.

bucks: Dollars.

red-handed: Caught doing something bad.

bad egg: A bad or dishonest person.

Practice

1. He looks like a million _____ these days.

2. I get a _____ any time I deal with that certain customer at work.

3. My mom is pretty relaxed but she would have a big _____ every once in a while.

4. Tony got fired after his boss caught him stealing _____.

5. He got a _____ raise at work. Lucky guy!

6. My teammate keeps _____ and always seems to forget that I set him up for most of his goals.

7. Getting a D on that test was a _____.

8. I can't just _____. I'm still in love with my ex-boyfriend.

9. That last project was _____ before I quit.

10. My mom is _____. She's gone on strike!

11. One _____ can negatively influence an entire company.

Answers

1. bucks

2. bee in my bonnet

3. blow-up

4. red-handed

5. massive

6. stealing my thunder

7. tough pill to swallow

8. get over it

9. the straw that broke the camel's back

10. sick and tired of it

11. bad egg

Confusing Words: Adverse/Averse

Both of these words indicate difficult (sometimes dangerous) conditions that make success or development hard. Both words sound similar.

Listening/pronunciation tip: Listen for the "d" sound to distinguish between the two words. You can also listen for where the syllable stress is placed:

- AD-verse has the first syllable stressed, the second is soft/weak

- a-VERSE has the emphasis stressed on the second part of the word, "-verse"

adverse: An adjective that usually relates to things and means harmful or unfavourable conditions for an action or person/people/animals, etc. "Adversity" is the noun form.

Approving this development will have an adverse impact on the animals that live there.

People are going to have an adverse reaction to him keeping his job. We need to fire him.

You may have some adverse side effects with this medication.

I overcame a lot of adversity to finally finish college.

averse: An adjective that usually applies to people and means a feeling or distaste or dislike; opposition to something. "Aversion" is the noun form.

My son is averse to eating vegetables of any kind.

I'm not averse to hiring another person, but you'll have to show me the numbers.

I think my kids are averse to doing the dishes. I have to threaten them to do it.

I have a strong aversion to doing laundry!

84

Practice

1. Did you experience any _____ effects from the vaccine?

2. Honestly, I'm _____ to kids. It's not my idea of fun to go on vacation with them.

3. I have an _____ to work.

4. My boss is _____ to people coming early and leaving early. We all stick to the 9-5.

5. I'm worried about the _____ impact that lots of mandatory overtime will have on employee morale.

6. I experienced a lot of _____ when I decided to go back to work as a single mom. It was so difficult.

Answers

1. adverse

2. averse

3. aversion

4. averse

5. adverse

6. adversity

Speaking practice: After checking your fill-in-the-blank answers, try speaking each sentence to a friend. Or, record yourself speaking each sentence on your smartphone. Then listen and see if your pronunciation is clear and easy to understand.

The Last Straw

Jerry is talking to Linda about wanting to leave his wife.

Jerry: So I think I'm going to **leave my wife**.

Linda: On no! What happened? You guys always seemed like pretty **happy campers** to me.

Jerry: Well, **the last straw** was looking at my retirement accounts and seeing that most of them were **cleaned out**. Plus, we're in the red on all our other accounts too. She loves to **shop till she drops** but I didn't realize how **dire** it was until now.

Linda: Sorry to hear that. I hope you can get back **in the black**. You went **from rags to riches** once. I'm sure you can do it again.

Jerry: Hopefully, but after paying the divorce lawyers, I'll have a lot of work to **make up for lost time** on those retirement accounts. And she may also want **spousal support.**

Linda: Well, hang in there my friend. I'm here for you.

Vocabulary

the last straw: The final annoying thing before someone loses their patience. For example, a child has been misbehaving all day but his dad finally yelled at him when he wouldn't stay in his room at bedtime.

in the black: To not be in debt.

leave my wife: Separate or get a divorce.

happy campers: People that are joyful or having fun together.

cleaned out: Usually refers to money, when someone spends everything.

shop till she drops: Loves shopping and spends lots of time doing it.

dire: Very bad.

make up for lost time: Wasted time that you can't get back.

spousal support: Money paid to a former husband or wife after getting divorced.

from rags to riches: Poor to rich.

Practice

1. The food situation is now becoming _____. One of us has to go shopping!

2. Honestly, this is _____ before he gets fired.

3. We started living frugally and are now _____.

4. I want to _____. We just don't have that much in common anymore.

5. The kids were such _____ when I bought them a new trampoline.

6. My wife loves to _____ but I feel nervous about how much money she's spending.

7. I had to pay _____ after getting divorced.

8. I only started dating in my twenties. Now, I have to _____.

9. Wow! I love the story of that guy going _____ when he moved to the USA.

Answers

1. dire

2. the last straw

3. in the black

4. leave my wife

5. happy campers

6. shop till she drops

7. spousal support

8. make up for lost time

9. from rags to riches

Highly Effective

Jim and John are talking about managing money.

Jim: Hey John. I'm wondering how you and Tina manage your money? It's a **key issue** for Jen and I and we need to come up with a better system.

John: We've been **married for 20 years** now and have a **joint account**. What works for us is that we're **brutally honest** about what we spend our money on. We don't **keep secrets**.

Jim: You're married to a keeper. That's for sure. Jen is **between jobs** and I'm **worried sick** about it. We may have to **borrow money** from the bank to **pay the mortgage**.

John: Sorry to hear that. When **money was tight** for us, we found a **highly effective** budgeting system. It could work for you.

Vocabulary

key issue: The most important thing.

married for _____ years: Number of years after a wedding that two people are together.

joint account: A bank account that two or more people hold together.

brutally honest: Holding nothing back from each other; no secrets.

keep secrets: Not telling important information.

between jobs: Describes someone who lost a job but is looking for another one.

worried sick: Anxious or stressed out to the extreme.

borrow money: Get a loan.

money was tight: Not enough money.

highly effective: Describes something that works very well.

Practice

1. Tony and I have been _____.

2. Can I be _____ with you? This partnership just isn't working out for us.

3. I don't want to _____ from each other anymore. It makes our relationship difficult.

4. Tim always seems to be _____. I wonder what's up with him?

5. _____ when I was going to medical school.

6. I know that you're _____ about it but get some sleep.

7. I've heard that it's a _____ system for losing weight.

8. Why don't we open up a _____? It would make things easier.

9. Let's try to _____ to make it through these next few weeks.

Answers

1. married for 10 years

2. brutally honest

3. keep secrets

4. between jobs

5. money was tight

6. worried sick

7. highly effective

8. joint account

9. borrow money

Hit the Books

Jerry is talking to Linda about having to study for an exam.

Jerry: I've been **breaking out in a cold sweat** a lot lately. I'm not used to having to **hit the books**.

Linda: What are you studying for?

Jerry: I have to pass this exam for work and I'll lose my job if I don't. I'm maybe **making a mountain of a molehill** but I can't help being nervous about it. It's been so long since I've had to take a test.

Linda: It's **like riding a bike**. You'll get back into it once you start. **Go with the flow**.

Jerry: Do you have any **study tips**?

Linda: My best advice is to study a little bit every day instead of **pulling all-nighters** or **cramming**. That doesn't work.

Vocabulary

breaking out in a cold sweat: To be afraid or nervous about something.

hit the books: When someone spends time studying.

go with the flow: To relax and go along with whatever.

making a mountain out of a molehill: To make something into a bigger deal than it is. For example, someone who loses sleep over a small problem.

like riding a bike: Something that you always remember how to do, even with a large break in between.

study tips: Ideas for how to study more effectively.

pulling all-nighters: Staying up all night to study or work.

cramming: Trying to learn everything for a test at the last minute.

Practice

1. Dude, sorry I can't hang out. I need to _____.

2. You'll get the hang of it. It's _____.

3. Before the second date, I kept _____. That's a bad sign, right?

4. I think you need to _____ with this school project. It sounds like you're taking it way more seriously than the other people in your group.

5. I don't think that _____ is a very effective study method.

6. One of the best _____ is to do it for one hour and then take a 10-minute break.

7. My days of _____ are over. I'm too old for that!

8. I think you're _____. It's not a big deal!

Answers

1. hit the books

2. like riding a bike

3. breaking out in a cold sweat

4. go with the flow

5. cramming

6. study tips

7. pulling all-nighters

8. making a mountain out of a molehill

Idioms #4

Butterflies in my stomach

Other forms: Butterflies in her/her stomach. Butterflies in our/their stomachs (less common because you have to assume that a group of people is all feeling the same).

Meaning: Nervous or anxious feeling about something. Often used to describe people before a test, presentation, job interview, performance, sports event, etc.

Origin: Unknown but seen as early as 1908.

Examples:

I have butterflies in my stomach just thinking about that exam.

She always gets butterflies in her stomach before doing a presentation.

We had butterflies in our stomachs before going on stage.

Extra practice:

List five situations in which people might get butterflies in their stomachs.

Blow off some steam

Other forms: Blowing/blew/blows off some steam (depends on the grammar in the sentence)

Meaning: To release or vent thoughts or feelings, that build up pressure/stress in your mind, through loud talking or strong action. For example, venting loudly about something frustrating. Or, having some drinks at a pub after a tough day at work.

Origin: Comes from the early days of railroads. Trains had no safety valves then so engineers would have to release or blow off some steam to prevent an explosion.

Examples:

Don't worry about him—he's just blowing off some steam.

Let's grab a beer after work and blow off some steam.

I blew off some steam this weekend by going to the batting cages.

Extra practice:

What are some ways that you like to blow off some steam?

Bang for the buck

Other forms: None.

Meaning: Something that offers good value for the money you paid for it.

Origin: First came from the late 1960s military language for expenditure for firepower.

bang = quality of materials/performance or use

buck = money

Could be a play on Pepsi's advertising campaign from the 1950s, "More bounce to the ounce."

Examples:

We need to get more bang for our buck. Mason just isn't worth what we're paying him. I though he was supposed to be the best. So far, I haven't been impressed.

That video game console isn't cheap but you get a lot of bang for the buck with all the games that come with it.

Mac computers aren't cheap but you get more bang for the buck. They're easier to use and last forever.

Extra practice:

What's something that you've bought recently which you felt like had a lot of bang for the buck?

Counting her chickens before they hatch

Other forms: Counting his/their/our/your chickens they hatch.

Meaning: Counting on something before it's already happened. For example, making plans to go to a certain university before getting the official acceptance letter. Often used to warn people who have possibly unrealistic hopes or expectations.

Origin: First seen in the 1500s in Thomas Howell's New Sonnets and Pretty Pamphlets. Could have originated from medieval or Latin fables. Not all eggs hatch into chicks. Some are unfertilized or have another problem.

Examples:

He got a loan for a car and a lottery ticket that he hoped would give him the money for monthly payments. He was 100% counting his chickens before they hatched.

She was counting her chickens before they hatched even though I told her to wait.

We can't count our chickens before they hatch. Just wait and see if this deal goes through. That supplier can still back out.

Extra practice:

Do you know anybody who counted their chickens before they hatched? What was the result of that situation?

A tough pill to swallow

Other forms: A bitter pill to swallow.

Meaning: Something difficult to get over or accept.

Origin: First seen in the 1600s. Probably related to medicine pills that can be big or bitter when you have to swallow them.

Examples:

Getting fired was a tough pill to swallow.

A D+ on that paper? That's a tough pill to swallow. I worked so hard on it.

Honestly, it was a bitter pill to swallow. I had no idea that Keith had so much debt until we were married.

Extra practice:

Have you ever been in a situation where there was a tough pill to swallow?

Affordable Housing

Kerry and Joe are talking about the housing situation in Vancouver.

Kerry: Did you hear that the city of Vancouver is **taking action** to address **housing prices**?

Joe: What are they doing? I'd love to move but **affordable housing** is hard to come by.

Kerry: They're building a new **housing development** and offering **low-interest rate** mortgages.

Joe: **It's about time**. Unless you **inherit money**, it's almost impossible for the **working Joe** to buy a house here.

Kerry: Well, **check into it** and if you buy one, invite me to your **housewarming party**!

Vocabulary

taking action: Doing something.

housing prices: The average price of houses in an area.

affordable housing: Housing that is designed to be cheaper than normal, usually subsidized by the government.

housing development: An area in which the houses have all been planned and built at the same time in an organized way.

low-interest rates: When interest rates are lower than normal.

it's about time: Finally.

inherit money: Getting money after someone has died.

working Joe: The average working person.

check into it: Find out more information about something.

housewarming party: A party after moving into a new home.

Practice

1. What are the average _____ in Victoria like?

2. Are you going to _____ when your parents die?

3. I've love to get into that new _____ in the west end of the city.

4. I'm happy that the city is finally _____ on that guy across the street.

5. There's no _____ in New York City.

6. Congratulations on your new place! When's the _____?

7. Did he finally do his chores? _____.

8. I'm just an average _____, doing the 9-5.

9. I'm not sure about that. I'll have to _____.

10. It's a great time to buy a house when there are _____.

Answers

1. housing prices

2. inherit money

3. housing development

4. taking action

5. affordable housing

6. housewarming party

7. it's about time

8. working Joe

9. check into it

10. low-interest rates

Famine

Sam and Carrie are talking about a famine.

Sam: Have you heard about the **famine** in ABC country?

Carrie: I have. It seems really bad, but I don't know much about it. Is it an **anomaly** or an **annual** thing?

Sam: Oh, it happens every year. Experts **attribute** it to XYZ country **diverting** and taking a **disproportionate** amount of water from the main river running through both countries.

Carrie: So frustrating and sad. Water shouldn't be a **finite** resource. Of course this would **impoverish** that country if it were happening every single year. We need to **augment** our financial aid to poorer countries.

Vocabulary

famine: Extreme lack of food (usually at the country level).

anomaly: Something that is not the norm.

annual: Occurring yearly.

attribute: Give credit to.

diverting: Change of course.

disproportionate: Too large or too smart compared to something else.

finite: Having an end or limit.

impoverish: To reduce to poverty.

augment: Increase, or make larger.

Practice

1. That _____ has killed hundreds of thousands of people so far.

2. Rich countries use a _____ amount of fossil fuels.

3. We won! It was kind of an _____. A small miracle.

4. The government didn't intend to _____ that whole group of people but that was the effect.

5. We have to stop _____ funds away from advertising. It's short-sighted.

6. Where are you going for your _____girl's trip?

7. We have _____ money. There has to be a way to reduce our budget each month.

8. You didn't come up with this idea on your own. You need to _____ it.

Answers

1. famine

2. disproportionate

3. anomaly

4. impoverish

5. diverting

6. annual

7. finite

8. attribute

Talking about a Company in Trouble

Jerry is talking to Linda about trouble at his company.

Jerry: My company has been **cutting corners** on this latest project and we're **in hot water**.

Linda: Well, honestly, it's time for your company to **face the music.** You've been doing some things that **cross the line** for years now. It's going to be **an uphill battle** for you.

Jerry: Hey, hey. I know. You're **barking up the wrong tree**! I don't have anything to do with making the decisions. I do what I'm told. I'm basically a **yes man.**

Linda: I know. But, I wish you'd find some **greener pastures**. That company is going to **go under** soon I think. Just **read between the lines.**

Jerry: Well, jobs in my field are like a **needle in a haystack** these days. I'd **pull the plug** if I could.

Vocabulary

cutting Corners: Doing something cheaply or badly. Can often be related to construction/home renovations.

face the music: Deal with the reality of something negative that you did. For example, getting punished for a crime.

in hot water: In trouble for something.

cross the line: Behave in an unacceptable way.

barking up the wrong tree: Blaming someone for something that isn't their fault.

greener pastures: A better opportunity someplace else.

go under: Go bankrupt or out of business.

yes man: A weak person who always agrees with their superior at work or in politics.

needle in a haystack: Something that is impossible to find.

an uphill battle: Something very difficult to deal with.

read between the lines: Discovering something secret or hidden.

pull the plug: Quit, or stop doing something.

Practice

1. That CEO made some terrible decisions and his company is about to _____.

2. I know you don't want to _____ but your company is about to go bankrupt.

3. I'm leaving my job and heading for _____.

4. It's time to _____ for ripping all those customers off.

5. Honestly, you're _____. Johnny did it, not me.

6. Donald Trump is _____ these days with the most recent scandal.

7. The guy painting my house is _____. I feel so angry about it.

8. I hate that my company likes to _____ on just about every deal they do.

9. I hate that my husband is forced into being a _____ in his new role at the company.

10. Looking for my glasses in my messy house is like finding a _____.

11. Quite honestly, it's going to be _____ to get back on track.

12. I think he's going to _____. That new guy just isn't performing well.

Answers

1. go under

2. read between the lines

3. greener pastures

4. face the music

5. barking up the wrong tree

6. in hot water

7. cutting corners

8. cross the line

9. yes man

10. needle in a haystack

11. an uphill battle

12. pull the plug

Dumped

Alex got dumped by his girlfriend.

John: Hey **bro**, what's up? You don't look so good.

Alex: I just got **dumped** by Kendra. And just when we started talking about **getting hitched.**

John: Sorry to hear that. Wasn't she super **flakey** though, always cancelling at the last minute?

Alex: Yeah, and I **straight up** caught her lying to me more than a few times.

John: Better off without her. Let's get **ripped** this weekend. It'll take your mind off of it.

Alex: Yeah, I want to **blow off some steam**. Just don't post about it on social media. I don't want to get **busted** by my boss. He just **added me** as a friend on Facebook.

Vocabulary

bro: A way to greet a close male friend (if you're also a guy).

dumped: Broken up with.

getting hitched: Getting married.

flakey: Describes someone who doesn't follow through with what they say or always cancels plans.

straight up: Speaking honestly.

ripped: Drunk.

blow off some steam: Relax; let loose.

added me: Becoming friends with someone on social media.

Practice

1. What do you like to do to _____?

2. I'll never work on another project with her if I can avoid it. She's so _____.

3. I got _____ last night at the work Christmas party. I hope that I didn't do anything too embarrassing.

4. Did you hear that Ted _____ Lindsay?

5. My grandma just _____ on Instagram. It's so cute!

6. I _____ never want to talk to that guy again.

7. Tom and I are _____ next month.

8. Hey _____, how are you doing these days?

Answers

1. blow off some steam

2. flakey

3. ripped

4. dumped

5. added me

6. straight up

7. getting hitched

8. bro

Talking About a Possible Strike

Jeremy and Rachel think that some workers at their company may go on strike.

Jeremy: I think the **blue-collar** workers at our company are going to **go on strike**.

Rachel: I get that feeling too. Management needs to **make some concessions** but I'm not sure they're willing to. Their benefits aren't in line with other workers in this industry.

Jeremy: Hopefully the two sides can **meet in the middle**. It's not like we're **stinking rich** and have **money burning a hole in our pocket**.

Rachel: Anyway, negotiations better **pan out** or we'll be **back to square one**.

Vocabulary

blue-collar: Describes a worker who does manual labour.

go on strike: Stop working to demand better job conditions.

make some concessions: Agree to, or give something to end a disagreement.

meet in the middle: When two sides both compromise to reach an agreement.

stinking rich: Describes someone who has an excessive amount of money.

money burning a hole in our pocket: Extra money you want to spend.

pan out: Work out.

back to square one: Starting at the beginning again.

Practice

1. We'll be _____ if we can't figure this bug out.

2. I think you can _____ and stop fighting about this.

3. If your job doesn't ____, you're always welcome back here.

4. My wife and I have some _____ and are thinking about buying a boat.

5. _____ workers can make some good money in Canada.

6. Let's _____ and end this sooner rather than later.

7. He's _____. Look at his house!

8. They're going to _____ if we don't pay them more.

Answers

1. back to square one

2. meet in the middle

3. pan out

4. money burning a hole in our pocket

5. blue-collar

6. make some concessions

7. stinking rich

8. go on strike

Comprehension Questions

1. What is the main concern that Jeremy and Rachel are discussing?

2. According to Jeremy, which group of workers does he believe is likely to go on strike?

3. What does Rachel suggest management needs to do to avoid a strike?

4. According to Jeremy, what is his hope for the outcome of the situation?

5. How does Jeremy describe the financial situation of the people involved in the conversation?

6. In Rachel's opinion, what is the current state they'll be in if negotiations fail?

7. What does Jeremy imply about the company's financial status?

8. How do Jeremy and Rachel feel about the possibility of a strike?

Answers

1. The main concern that Jeremy and Rachel are discussing is the possibility of workers at their company going on strike.

2. Jeremy believes that the blue-collar workers at their company are likely to go on strike.

3. Rachel suggests that management needs to make concessions to address the workers' concerns and improve their benefits, which are not in line with industry standards.

4. Jeremy hopes that the two sides can meet in the middle to avoid a strike.

5. Jeremy describes their financial situation by saying, "It's not like we're stinking rich and have money burning a hole in our pocket."

6. If negotiations don't work out, Rachel believes they'll be back to square one.

7. Jeremy implies that they are not stinking rich and do not have money readily

available.

8. Jeremy and Rachel seem concerned about the possibility of a strike, and both express a hope for successful negotiations to avoid the situation.

Discussion Questions

1. How do you believe open communication between employees and management can contribute to a positive work environment?

2. In your opinion, what are some effective strategies for resolving conflicts in the workplace, especially when it involves differing perspectives on benefits and concessions?

3. How do you think financial considerations impact workplace dynamics and employee satisfaction in general? Can you provide examples of situations where financial factors influenced decisions in a work setting?

4. Reflecting on the importance of industry standards in the workplace, how can companies ensure that their employee benefits remain competitive and aligned with broader industry norms? What role does benchmarking play in this process?

5. When it comes to negotiations in any context, what are some key principles or strategies that can lead to mutually beneficial outcomes? How can both parties find common ground and avoid potential conflicts?

Finishing Work for the Day

Jerry and Linda are going to get some dinner after work.

Jerry: I'm so tired. Let's **call it a day** and grab some dinner. It's **my treat**.

Linda: Sure, I'd love to but only if we **go Dutch**. You **foot the bill** for me too often!

Jerry: Sure, if you insist. Let's check out that dessert place. They have sandwiches and then I can satisfy my **sweet tooth**. It's expensive but **worth it** I think.

Linda: Okay, **twist my arm**. Let's go. And don't just pick up the bill when I'm in the bathroom. I want to **pony up** for my share, okay?

Jerry: Let's **make a break for it** before **the big cheese** finds more work for us to do!

Linda: Sure, let's **head out**.

Vocabulary

call it a day: To stop working for the rest of the day.

foot the bill: To pay for.

go Dutch: Each person pays their own bill, especially at a restaurant or bar.

pony up: To get money/credit cards out to pay for something.

worth it: Good enough to justify the high cost.

twist my arm: Convince to do something.

sweet tooth: To like sugary foods.

my treat: To offer to pay, usually for a meal or drink.

make a break for it: Leave somewhere quickly.

the big cheese: The boss.

head out: To go somewhere.

Practice

1. I feel uncomfortable when guys pay for me so I insist that we _____.

2. It's time to _____ for all those drinks you had!

3. I have a wicked _____ and can't stop eating candy.

4. Is the company going to _____ for the Christmas party this year?

5. Let's _____. I'm beat.

6. It's time to _____ and go home while the boss isn't looking.

7. Let's grab lunch. _____.

8. I hope to be _____ one day!

9. I'm tired. I'm going to _____ now.

10. Okay, I know that subscription box is expensive but it's _____ to me.

11. I didn't want to do it! My wife had to _____ to get me to go skydiving with her.

Answers

1. go Dutch

2. pony up

3. sweet tooth

4. foot the bill

5. call it a day

6. make a break for it

7. my treat

8. the big cheese

9. head out

10. worth it

11. twist my arm

The Chicken or the Egg

Bob and Sam are talking about Sam's son.

Bob: Hey, how's your son doing these days? I heard he got into a bit of trouble?

Sam: He **drives me up the wall**. He's both a **slacker** and a **stoner.** I don't know if it's **the chicken or the egg** but whatever the case, he's **flunking** out of high school because he's always **high**.

Bob: You were such a **keener** in school. How did this happen?

Sam: Trust me. I have no idea.

Bob: What does he say when you talk to him?

Sam: He just yells, "**Get off my back**!" We can't even have a real conversation about it. I'm scared he's ruining his life.

Bob: Well, I'm here for you if you need to talk about things.

Vocabulary

drives me up the wall: Makes me crazy.

slacker: Describes someone who is lazy.

stoner: Describes someone who likes to do illegal drugs often.

the chicken or the egg: Which thing comes first?

flunking: Failing.

high: On drugs.

keener: Describes someone who is the opposite of lazy.

get off my back: Stop bugging me.

Practice

1. Seriously, _____. I don't want to talk about this anymore.

2. It _____ when he doesn't put his dishes in the dishwasher.

3. You're such a _____, studying two weeks before the test.

4. Is it _____? It's difficult to tell in this situation.

5. Let's get _____ after work tonight.

6. I was a _____ in high school but I quit when I went to university.

7. I'm _____ math but I don't care.

8. My daughter is a _____ and doesn't care about school. She'd rather just hang around with her friends.

Answers

1. get off my back

2. drives me up the wall

3. keener

4. the chicken or the egg

5. high

6. stoner

7. flunking

8. slacker

Brush Up

Ethan is talking to his friend about how stressed out he is.

Ethan: I'm feeling stressed out. I think I **bit off more than I can chew**.

Jeremiah: Yeah? What's up? Whatever it is, I'm sure that you can **pull it off.**

Ethan: Well, I had to **brush up on** new programming language for a project I'm doing in one of my classes but I'm not **catching on** as quickly as I usually do. The homework is starting to **pile up.** It's pure **drudgery**.

Jeremiah: Don't **freak out.** You're a smart guy! **Get on it** and you'll be **up to speed** in no time. Soon, you'll be **showing off** like usual. Haha!

Ethan: Not likely but thanks for your support. I want to **leave this behind** me as soon as possible!

Vocabulary

bit off more than I can chew: Choosing to do something that requires a lot more time and energy to do than you thought before starting the task.

pull it off: Succeed at doing something, usually difficult.

brush up on: Refresh; relearn something.

catching on: Understanding or figuring something out.

pile up: Not taking enough action so that projects or tasks increase to a stressful amount.

drudgery: Describes boring work.

freak out: Panic or feel extreme anxiety about something.

get on it: Start doing something.

up to speed: Describes someone who is fully informed or who has full knowledge.

showing off: Boasting or bragging.

leave this behind: Forget about it; finish it so I can forget about the stress.

Practice

1. Stop _____! I already know that you're good at that.

2. If anyone can _____, it's you.

3. Tommy is famous for letting assignments _____ and then pulling all-nighters.

4. I think she's _____ quickly. I'm so happy with her progress.

5. Can we please _____ us? We keep coming back to it but it's not helpful.

6. You'll get _____ here in a few months.

7. Math is pure _____ to me. I can't understand how some people find it interesting.

8. Okay, let's _____. We have so much to do.

9. Don't _____ about what I'm going to tell you, okay?

10. I need to _____ my high school math for this accounting class I'm taking.

11. I may have _____. I think I need some help with this big project if it's going to get done in time.

Answers

1. showing off

2. pull it off

3. pile up

4. catching on

5. leave this behind

6. up to speed

7. drudgery

8. get on it

9. freak out

10. brush up on

11. bit off more than I can chew

Idioms #5

Blow the whistle

Other forms: Blew the whistle (depends on the grammar in the sentence).

Meaning: To expose fraud, corruption, unethical conduct of a person, group, or institution/company, etc. to an authority. The term whistleblower is used for the person who does this and they do it at great personal risk to themselves.

Origin: People used to blow whistles to get the attention of police.

Examples:

I know you don't want to but I think you should blow the whistle on that politician. He's so sketchy and people really deserve to know what happens behind the scenes in his office.

It's time for someone to blow the whistle on that corrupt police chief. The officers should really stand up to him.

I blew the whistle on my boss. It was time for the CEO to know about her harassment.

Extra practice:

Are there any famous whistleblowers in your country?

Fall through the cracks

Other forms: Fell/falling/falls through the cracks (depends on the grammar in the sentence).

Meaning: When someone or something isn't seen, helped, or included with others. The "cracks" are the failures of attention or a system like a social welfare system that has flaws in its design or performance so that people like war veterans' needs are failed.

Origin: Unknown. However, it's easy to imagine small cracks in old wooden floors and things going missing.

Examples:

Please don't let this proposal fall through the cracks. It's too important.

I'm worried about this falling through the cracks, so let's make a note in our calendars to check on our progress in two weeks

Sorry, your request fell through the cracks and we didn't get to it. Let me take a look at it now.

Extra practice:

What falls through the cracks in your life when you get really busy?

Crack the whip

Other forms: Cracked/cracks/cracking the whip (depends on the grammar in the sentence).

Meaning: Speaking or acting in a very strict or harsh way that tries to force others to do what you need/want. Often used in a negative sense in that people have been lazy although it can be used in a light-hearted manner among friends or people who like each other.

Origin: Related to drivers of horse-drawn carriages who cracked their whips to get the horses to go faster. The first use of it related to people is seen in the 1800s.

Examples:

Let's crack the whip! It's time for everyone go get back to work. They can't keep taking 2-hour lunches.

Sorry everyone. I have to crack the whip! We're not going to finish before the pizza arrives if we don't get to work.

My teacher is cracking the whip these days. She gets angry if we don't finish our homework on time.

Extra practice:

Did your parents use to crack the whip when you were a kid? What about?

Barking up the wrong tree

Other forms: None.

Meaning: Someone who is wrong about the reason for something or how to do something.

Origin: From the 1800s in the USA where hunting dogs would bark at the base of a tree when they thought a wild animal like a racoon was in it so that their owners could shoot it. But, the wild animal had sometimes had already escaped which left the dogs barking at the wrong tree.

Examples:

Joe keeps sending Susan flowers to try and seduce her. He's so barking up the wrong tree —she loves chocolates, not flowers.

Amy really wants to go out with John, but she's barking up the wrong tree—John doesn't like her at all, but Martin has liked her for years.

Don't you think that Ted is barking up the wrong tree? Why is he blaming our team for the bad sales results this quarter? We've done better than ever.

Extra practice:

Have you ever been blamed for something that you didn't do?

Feeling the pinch

Other forms: Felt the pinch (to talk about the past).

Meaning: Experiencing financial difficulties. Could be related to companies, schools, organizations, people, etc.

Origin: From the 1800s. Could be related to having to tighten a belt when there is less food to eat. Or, kids who have to wear shoes that are too small and get their toes pinched because their parents can't afford to buy new ones.

Examples:

My company is feeling the pinch since we lost a bunch of accounts due to Covid-19.

I've been feeling the pinch since my husband lost his job.

Extra practice:

Did people in your country feel the pinch during Covid-19?

Bend over backwards

Other forms: Bending/bends/bent over backwards (depends on the grammar in the sentence).

Meaning: Work extra hard; go out of your way to do something special for someone. Used in a negative sense in that this hard work isn't rewarded.

Origin: From the 900s. Refers to a gymnast bending his back which is not that easy to do unless you're very flexible.

Examples:

I bent over backwards for that company but still got fired.

I'm so tired of Tim bending over backwards but never getting a raise at work.

My wife bends over backwards for the kids and they just walk all over her.

Extra practice:

Do you ever bend over backwards for people? In what situations do you do that?

At death's door

Other forms (less common): At death's doorstep. On death's doorstep.

Meaning: Close to dying. Used quite informally. For example, a doctor would never say that a relative of your is, "At death's door."

Origin: Death and an entryway (door) became associated with each other in England in the 1300s. At death, some people think that you go through a door of some kind to the next life.

Examples:

My friend is at death's door. I'm not sure she's going to make it.

My grandpa was at death's door for months but he surprisingly recovered.

When I was sick with Covid-19, I was on death's doorstep. I had to go to the hospital and was on a ventilator for weeks. I think everyone had given up on me.

Extra practice:

Do you know anyone who is, or has been at death's door for a while?

Break a Leg

Linda is talking to Jerry about a play that she'll be in next month.

Jerry: Hey, I heard **through the grapevine** that you're going to be in a play next month.

Linda: It's true. I must admit! I had to **blow off some steam** from work and escaping into my character is a great way to do that.

Jerry: You're really **taking the bull by the horns** lately! Can I come watch?

Linda: Sure, **knock yourself out**! It's a little bit **amateur hour** but **on the upside**, the tickets are cheap!

Jerry: Okay, I'll come for sure. I can't forget to tell you to **break a leg** though!

Vocabulary

break a leg: To wish someone good luck, usually before performing or going on stage.

blow off some steam: Doing something to get rid of stress. For example, having a few drinks after a difficult work project.

knock yourself out: To try hard to do something. Often something that others think is a waste of time.

taking the bull by the horns: Doing something bravely and decisively.

through the grapevine: To spread information informally. Often related to gossip.

amateur hour: Not professional.

on the upside: Something positive in a generally negative situation.

Practice

1. I heard _____ that Tom and Monica broke up.

2. You want to do that for me? _____.

3. I starting playing soccer to _____ from my terrible job.

4. Well, _____, this job has better hours.

5. Good luck and _____.

6. It was hard to watch that presentation. Talk about _____.

7. I'm _____ at work lately and it's going well!

Answers

1. through the grapevine

2. Knock yourself out

3. blow off some steam

4. on the upside

5. break a leg

6. amateur hour

7. taking the bull by the horns

Lifestyle Changes

Kim is talking to Tanya about her health.

Kim: Did you **go to the doctor**? I know you were **not feeling well**.

Tanya: I did. She didn't **diagnose me** with anything but said that I'd need to make some serious **lifestyle changes**. My **overall health** is quite poor.

Kim: Oh no! What did she recommend?

Tanya: She said that I have to **reduce my stress**, **get plenty of sleep**, and **eat a balanced diet**.

Kim: That doesn't sound so bad. Do you have to **quit smoking**?

Tanya: Oh yeah, that too. It **shook me up**. She said that if I didn't change, my **life expectancy** would decrease.

Vocabulary

go to the doctor: Have an appointment with a doctor.

not feeling well: Feeling sick.

diagnose me: Assign a name to a health problem.

lifestyle changes: Change in what you eat, how much you exercise and other unhealthy habits like smoking or drinking alcohol.

overall health: General level of healthiness/unhealthiness.

reduce my stress: Decrease the amount of stress in your life.

get plenty of sleep: Sleep eight hours a night.

eat a balanced diet: Eating mostly healthy food from all the food groups.

quit smoking: Stop using cigarettes.

shook me up: Made me feel nervous, worried, or anxious.

life expectancy: How long you can expect to live.

Practice

1. In Canada, the average _____ for men is 84 years.

2. Please _____. It seems like you've been sick for a while now.

3. You'll have to make some _____ to reduce your chance of a heart attack.

4. It _____ when he told me that he wanted to get divorced.

5. I'm _____. I need to go home early today.

6. I hope that I can _____ by changing jobs.

7. My goal is to _____ this year but I know it won't be easy.

8. Please try to _____ if you want to lower your cholesterol.

9. My doctor didn't _____ with anything but just said that I had to stop drinking so much coffee.

10. His _____ is quite good, considering how old he is.

11. Please try to _____ before your exam. You'll be able to think more clearly.

Answers

1. life expectancy

2. go to the doctor

3. lifestyle changes

4. shook me up

5. not feeling well

6. reduce my stress

7. quit smoking

8. eat a balanced diet

9. diagnose me

10. overall health

11. get plenty of sleep

Goofing Around

Andy and Matt are talking about their kids.

Andy: How's it going these days?

Matt: Oh, I'm feeling like I might **snap** at any moment. My kids alternate between **goofing around** and **beating each other up.** I wish they'd **cut it out** and act normally.

Andy: That sounds tough. They'll **grow up** before you know it though! Enjoy it while they're young.

Matt: I know that but they **wear me down.** I hate **dealing with** their battles.

Andy: Lighten up a little! Let them **battle it out**. I know it's bad but I let my kids **get away with** murder! It helps me stay sane.

Vocabulary

snap: Get suddenly angry.

goofing around: Being silly or joking with someone.

beating each other up: Hitting or being physically violent towards each other.

cut it out: Stop doing something.

grow up: Get bigger or older.

wear me down: Make me feel tired and weary.

dealing with: Handling.

lighten up: Relax; not take things so seriously.

battle it out: Fight until there's a winner.

get away with: To do something bad but not receive punishment for it.

Practice

1. I'm not sure you should get in between them. Why not let them _____?

2. My kids _____! I need to take a walk every day to get a break.

3. Hey, stop _____. We need to get some things done.

4. You should _____. It'll be better for your mental health.

5. Kids _____ so quickly.

6. I'm going to _____ if you don't stop that.

7. The pen tapping annoys me. Please _____.

8. I know you're _____ a lot right now. Can I help by watching your kids tonight?

9. Do you think we can _____ it? I'm worried that we won't.

10. My cat and dog love _____.

Answers

1. battle it out

2. wear me down

3. goofing around

4. lighten up

5. grow up

6. snap

7. cut it out

8. dealing with

9. get away with

10. beating each other up

Negotiating with Another Company

Ken and Bob are talking about some negotiations.

Ken*:* I wanted to **touch base** with you and find out where you're at with that new software we recommend to your company.

Bob: Oh you know Jerry. He likes to **take things slowly** and is reluctant to **shake things up**. What we're currently using is fine for now he thinks. Sorry if I gave you **the wrong impression** that this deal might happen quickly.

Ken*:* To **go out on a limb** here, if you don't upgrade, you'll likely be **playing catch up** for years **down the road**.

Bob: Big picture, we know that. Unfortunately, I don't **call the shots** or **hold the purse strings**. Jerry does.

Vocabulary

touch base: To check in with someone.

take things slowly: To not move quickly.

shake things up: To reorganize something in a drastic or big way.

the wrong impression: To think wrongly about someone, based on a first meeting.

go out on a limb: To take a risk.

playing catch up: To try to reach the same level as others, especially after starting late.

down the road: In the future.

big picture: Considering everything.

call the shots: To make the decisions.

hold the purse strings: To make the financial decisions.

Practice

1. You'll have to talk to Tommy about money stuff. I don't _____.

2. I'm afraid that you've got _____ about our company.

3. Things are fine now but I'm worried about what will happen _____.

4. If we don't upgrade our databases, we'll be _____.

5. I only _____ about HR related things.

6. Can we _____ next week? I'd love to hear how you're doing.

7. My CEO wants to _____ in terms of the kind of people we hire.

8. I don't want to _____ too much here, but someone has to tell you this.

9. I'm a mover and shaker but my boss likes to _____.

10. I know you don't agree with me but I don't think you're looking at the _____.

Answers

1. hold the purse strings

2. the wrong impression

3. down the road

4. playing catch up

5. call the shots

6. touch base

7. shake things up

8. go out on a limb

9. take things slowly

10. big picture

Bite the Bullet

Jerry is talking to Linda about buying a car.

Jerry: Hey Linda, so I decided to finally **bite the bullet** and get a new car.

Linda: Oh wow! Did it **break the bank**?

Jerry: Kind of, but I didn't want another **lemon**.

Linda*:* I know, **when it rains, it pours,** right? Your car was always in the shop!

Jerry*:* For real. It was so annoying. Now, I just have to **crack the whip** on my employees to get out there and make more money for me to pay for it.

Linda*:* Don't **discredit** yourself! You're **working your fingers to the bone** too.

Vocabulary

bite the bullet: Doing something that you've been avoiding for a while. For example, someone finally deciding to paint their house after delaying for years.

when it rains, it pours: When more than one bad thing happens at the same time.

crack the whip: To be tough on someone.

break the bank: Something that costs a lot.

a lemon: A reference to a car that needs more repairs than usual.

discredit: Not give someone credit.

working your fingers to the bone: Working very hard, beyond capacity.

Practice

1. I wish he'd just _____ and stop complaining so much!

2. My mom used to _____ and make us all clean the house every Sunday morning.

3. That guy has the worst luck! _____.

4. I hope this new-to-me car I just bought isn't _____.

5. Let's go on a nice vacation but I don't want to _____.

6. I don't want to _____ his success, but his father handed him the job.

7. Take a break Tom! You're _____ lately.

Answers

1. bite the bullet

2. crack the whip

3. When it rain, it pours

4. a lemon

5. break the bank

6. discredit

7. working your fingers to the bone

126

Bitter Divorce

Sierra and Brian are talking about their friends getting divorced.

Sierra: Did you **hear the news**? Jeremy and Katie are going through a **bitter divorce**.

Brian: Really? What about the kids? Are they doing **joint custody** or **sole custody**?

Sierra: Joint custody. Jeremy will have them **on weekends** but he has to **pay child support**.

Brian: Poor kids. That was a pretty **dysfunctional family** and they've already had a **troubled childhood**.

Sierra: A **broken home** might be better than all that conflict though. It's too bad that Jeremy and Katie aren't **on good terms**.

Vocabulary

hear the news: Catch the latest gossip.

bitter divorce: A divorce that is hostile with both people feeling angry towards the other.

joint custody: When divorced parents each spend some time taking care of their children.

sole custody: When a divorced parent is responsible 100% of the time for the children.

on weekends: On Saturday and Sunday.

pay child support: When one divorced parent has to give money to the other parent to help pay for the care of the children.

dysfunctional family: A family with many problems.

troubled childhood: Growing up in a family or situation with a lot of problems.

broken home: A home where the parents are divorced.

on good terms: Friendly and get along well.

Practice

1. Thankfully my former boss and I are _____. I need him for a reference.

2. I grew up in a _____ but have worked hard to overcome this.

3. Alex and Jen seem to be doing well with their _____ agreement.

4. Did you _____ ? Jeremy cheated on his wife.

5. _____, I like to spend as much time outside as possible.

6. He's had a _____ so far. I'm surprised that he still does well at school.

7. I want to get _____ of the kids. Tom is a terrible father.

8. I grew up in a _____ and have tried my best to make things better for my kids.

9. I had such a _____ but I'm happy that I don't have to see him anymore.

10. She does _____ but it should be way more than $500 a month I think.

Answers

1. on good terms

2. broken home

3. joint custody

4. hear the news

5. on weekends

6. troubled childhood

7. sole custody

8. dysfunctional family

9. bitter divorce

10. pay child support

128

Giving Someone the Cold Shoulder

Jerry is talking Linda about his daughter.

Jerry: My daughter called me for the first time **in ages**. She usually **gives me the cold shoulder**.

Linda: Why? What happened to your relationship?

Jerry: Well, we got in a big fight about paying for **grad school**. She was **counting her chickens before they hatch** and assumed I would pay. But, I just didn't have **the dough**. That new car I bought **cost a pretty penny**.

Linda: Yeah, my son only calls **once in a blue moon**. He usually wants some **moola** too! But to be fair, he never misses a Mother's Day card.

Jerry: Kids these days! That seems like the **bare minimum**!

Vocabulary

gives me the cold shoulder: To ignore someone.

once in a blue moon: Rarely.

counting her chickens before they hatch: Counting on something before it's already happened. For example, making plans to go to a certain university before getting the official acceptance letter.

in ages: In a long time.

grad school: Graduate school.

the dough: Money.

moola: Money.

bare minimum: The least someone is obligated to do.

cost a pretty penny: To be expensive.

Practice

1. I wish my kids would do more than the _____ to keep the house clean and tidy.

2. I haven't seen my parents _____ because of Covid.

3. I play tennis _____ because it's always rainy where I live.

4. My neighbour has been _____ lately but I'm not sure why.

5. My daughter is convinced that she'll get into Harvard but I keep telling her to stop _____.

6. I wish that I'd gone to _____ right after I'd finished university.

7. My brother makes the big _____.

8. Give me _____ please!

9. My university education _____. I hope it was worth it!

Answers

1. bare minimum

2. in ages

3. once in a blue moon

4. giving me the cold shoulder

5. counting her chicken before they hatch

6. grad school

7. moola

8. the dough

9. cost a pretty penny

Good With Computers

Terry is talking to Sienna about his computer problems.

Terry: Hey, you're **good with computer**s, right? I'm trying to write an essay that's due tomorrow, but my **computer freezes** every couple of minutes. And then . . .

Sienna: Hold on. First things first. Did you **shut down your computer** yet?

Terry: No, should I do that?

Sienna: Yes, and then **restart the computer**.

Terry: Okay, it says it's going to do some **scheduled maintenance** and **install updates**.

Sienna: Let that run and once it starts, do a **virus scan.** It should work a lot better now.

Vocabulary

good with computers: Describes someone who knows how to use computers well.

computer freezes: The computer operating system stops working. For example, you can't click anything on the computer screen

hold on: Wait.

first things first: Do the most important thing first before jumping ahead to other action/things.

shut down your computer: Turn off the computer.

restart the computer: Turn back on the computer after turning it off.

scheduled maintenance: Routine maintenance that helps a computer operating system function well.

install updates: This usually refers to a computer or other electronic device. Involves updating the software.

virus scan: A program that looks for harmful viruses on a computer.

Practice

1. Let's run a _____ first to see if we can catch any problems that way.

2. Just _____ a minute. Did you restart your computer? That's the first thing you should do.

3. Always _____ as soon as possible for your electronic devices to avoid problems.

4. Ted is _____. Let's ask him for some help.

5. _____. Let's get some snacks and drinks for our study session.

6. The network will be down for _____ tonight from 2 am to 4 am.

7. Did you _____ your computer yet? I think that might help.

8. I hate that my _____ at the worst possible times.

9. _____ before going home for the day. I want to save money on electricity.

Answers

1. virus scan

2. hold on

3. install updates

4. good with computers

5. first things first

6. scheduled maintenance

7. restart the computer

8. computer freezes

9. shut down your computer

Idioms #6

Food for thought

Other forms: None.

Meaning: Something to think about or an idea to consider. Can be used in a positive sense (What a great presentation! Lots of food for thought) but often used in a negative way when you disagree with someone about something or want to avoid further conversation (Well, that's some food for thought. Let me get back to you).

Origin: Unknown.

Examples:

Interesting idea. It's certainly some food for thought.

Thanks so much for your very interesting presentation. There was lots of food for thought in it.

It's certainly some food for thought but I don't think that I'm going to change my mind on this.

Extra practice:

Have you learned anything interesting lately? That's some food for thought!

Beat me to the punch

Other forms: Beating/beats me to the punch (depends on the grammar in the sentence).

Meaning: Say or do something before someone else.

Origin: From the early 1900s regarding boxing. Sometimes, it's possible to win with just one punch by knocking someone out before they even hit you.

Examples:

You beat me to the punch—that's exactly what I was going to say.

Oh wow. It looks like Apple is beating Samsung to the punch with eye recognition.

Tommy usually beats me to the punch on most things. He's a man of action!

Extra practice:

Has anyone ever beat you to the punch? What was the situation?

133

Give him the cold shoulder

Other forms: Giving/gives/gave her/them/us/me the cold shoulder. It can also be used in the receiving form (I got the cold shoulder from my boss).

Meaning: Ignore someone you know. Or, being treated in a cold and unfriendly manner by someone you know. Used in a very negative sense.

Origin: Somewhat unknown but could be from a mistranslation of a Latin phrase in Nehemiah 9:29 in the Vulgate Bible.

Examples:

I got the cold shoulder from my girlfriend when I forgot her birthday.

Let's give him the cold shoulder when he behaves that way and see if it makes a difference.

Terry gave me the cold shoulder when she saw me at my high school reunion. We used to be friends! It was so strange that he didn't want to talk to me.

Extra practice:

Have you ever given anyone the cold shoulder? Has anyone ever done that to you?

Crunch the numbers

Other forms: Crunched/crunches/crunching the numbers (depends on the grammar in the sentence).

Meaning: Informal way to say, "analyze data."

Origin: Came into use in the 1980s when computers became more commonplace and refers to the complicated numerical calculations that mainframe computers did at the time.

Examples:

Let's crunch the numbers and see if we can figure this out.

I crunched the numbers and it looks like we'll be $2000 over budget.

Tony is crunching the numbers right now. I think he should be done with the spreadsheet by the end of the day.

Extra practice:

Name 10 jobs where you have to crunch the numbers regularly.

A storm is brewing

Other forms: A storm was brewing (used to talk about difficulties or conflict in the past that happened before another event).

Meaning: A way to say that difficulty or danger is expected in the future. Describes a conflict between people.

Origin: Unknown but could be related to sailors reading the signs in the ocean and sky to predict a coming storm.

Examples:

I think a storm is brewing at work between Marnie and Carrie. Things are getting tenser by the day.

I'm worried that a storm is brewing between my parents. They keep complaining to me about each other.

A storm was brewing for a while. It was only a matter of time until it came to a head. Of course, Toni was going to find out that Ted cheated on her.

Extra practice:

Do you know anyone in your life where a storm is brewing?

Give them a run for their money

Other forms: Many forms are possible. For example:

- They always give us a run for our money.

- He gave us a run for our money.

- He's giving them a run for their money.

Meaning: Provide good competition. Usually refers to sports or business.

Origin: Could be from horse racing and placing bets. Sometimes horses are withdrawn from a race after bets are placed in which case you don't get a run for your money.

Examples:

I think we can give them a run for their money if we play well.

Wow! The Blue Jays gave the Yankees a run for their money.

That company is giving us a run for our money with their latest release. Let's make a new plan and see if we can't get back on top.

Extra practice:

Do you have a favorite sports team? Is there an example of when they gave another team a run for their money?

Eat your words

Other forms: Eating/ate/eats his/her/our/their words.

Meaning: To be forced to admit you were wrong about something. Often used to make a prediction about the future when you think someone is saying something ridiculous (He'll have to eat his words).

Origin: Uncertain but traced back to the 1500s.

Examples:

You're going to have to eat your words and apologize to your dad, I think.

Oh, she'll be eating her words soon. It's just a matter of time.

Don't worry too much about it. She'll eventually eat her words and take back what she said.

Extra practice:

Have you ever been forced to eat your words? What happened?

Save me a Seat

Jerry and Sid are talking about coming late to class.

Jerry: Hey Sid, can you **save me a seat** in class? I'm going to **come late**.

Sid: **Take your time**. I'll even **take notes** for you. But, why are you always late?

Jerry: You know the cute girls always catch my eye and then I have to stop and talk. But, **keep up the good work** my friend. I love that you always **pay attention** in class.

Sid: Will you ever **evolve** into a responsible student?! Anyway, we should **have lunch** after class. What do you think?

Jerry: Sounds great. **In light of** what a good friend you are, it's **my treat**.

Vocabulary

save me a seat: Hold a chair or spot for someone at an event, meeting, class, etc.

come late: Show up not on time.

take your time: Don't worry about hurrying.

take notes: Write down briefly what is being heard.

keep up the good work: Continue doing the good things you're doing.

pay attention: Look closely; focus.

have lunch: Eat lunch together.

evolve: Develop or improve to a better state; change for the better.

in light of: Taking into consideration.

my treat: I'll pay.

Practice

1. Do you want to _____ next Friday?

2. Please _____! You'll need to know this for your test next week.

3. Our company needs to _____ if we want to survive.

4. If you _____ to Dr. Kim's class, you have to sit in the front row.

5. Jeremy, _____. You did so well on your exam.

6. _____ this new information, we should have another meeting to discuss things.

7. Don't worry about the prices. It's _____.

8. Please _____. I'm going to be a little bit late getting there.

9. Please _____ for this meeting, okay?

10. _____ doing this test. You have two hours to do it. It's more than enough.

Answers

1. have lunch

2. pay attention

3. evolve

4. come late

5. keep up the good work

6. in light of

7. my treat

8. save me a seat

9. take notes

10. take your time

Breaking Out in a Cold Sweat

Tom is a mature student who is talking to Jackie about studying for an exam.

Tom: I've been **breaking out in a cold sweat** a lot lately. I'm **a bundle of nerves**. I'm not used to having to study so much.

Jackie: What are you studying for?

Tom: I have to pass this exam for work and I'll lose my job if I don't. I'm maybe **making a mountain of a molehill** but I can't help being nervous about it. It's been so long since I've had to take a test.

Jackie: It's **like riding a bike**. You'll get back into it once you start. **Go with the flow**.

Tom: Do you have any **study tips**?

Jackie: My best advice is to study a little bit every day instead of pulling all-nighters or **cramming**. That doesn't work. Give yourself time to **chew it over**.

Vocabulary

breaking out in a cold sweat: To be afraid or nervous about something.

a bundle of nerves: Describes someone who is very nervous or worried about something.

making a mountain out of a molehill: To make something into a bigger deal than it is. For example, someone who loses sleep over a small problem.

like riding a bike: Something that you always remember how to do, even with a large break in between.

go with the flow: To relax and go along with whatever happens.

study tips: Ideas for how to study more effectively.

cramming: Trying to learn everything for a test at the last minute.

chew it over: In this case, means taking time and not rushing when considering the test material.

Practice

1. You'll get the hang of it. It's _____.

2. This final exam has me _____. I'm so worried about it.

3. I think you need to _____ with this school project. It sounds like you're taking it way more seriously than the other people in your group.

4. I'll have to _____ for a for a few days. Can I let you know next week?

5. I don't think that _____ is a very effective study method.

6. You're _____ right now. Is anything wrong?

7. One of the best _____ is to do it for one hour and then take a 10-minute break.

8. I think you're _____. It's not a big deal!

Answers

1. like riding a bike

2. breaking out in a cold sweat

3. go with the flow

4. chew it over

5. cramming

6. a bundle of nerves

7. study tips

8. making a mountain out of a molehill

140

In the Pipeline

A student is commenting on climate change in a class.

I think that all our discussion about climate change **overlooks** one important thing— what we eat. **Cattle** production on **factory farms** releases a massive amount of **methane gas** into the atmosphere, not to mention polluting the local water sources. This is important because it's something that individuals can have an impact on and it's time to **come to grips with** this. We need to eat less meat!

The good news is that there is a shift happening in consumer awareness. More and more plant-based meats are **in the pipeline** and they are becoming increasingly popular with consumers. These new kinds of "meat" have the potential to **transform** the way we eat. I'm **under no illusion** that we'll suddenly have more Vegans because people are worried about climate change. However, plant-based meats **have a lot of potential** if two or three times a week, people choose it instead of beef, pork, or chicken. People would be healthier too!

Vocabulary

overlooks: Fails to notice something.

cattle: A name for cows (more than 1 of them).

factory farms: Large farms that operate on a huge scale.

methane gas: A kind of gas that's released by cows as they digest food.

come to grips with: Begin to deal with.

in the pipeline: something being developed by a person, company, government, etc. that will be available soon.

transform: Dramatic change.

under no illusion: False idea or belief.

have a lot of potential: Has the ability to change into something else in the future.

Practice

1. I'm _____ that this situation will get better.

2. The _____ outside my city pollute the air, land, and water.

3. We have to _____ the fact that climate change is real.

4. _____ is a major contributor to climate change.

5. I want to _____ this piece of land into an organic farm.

6. He _____ but he needs to focus on his studies instead of playing video games.

7. We have a similar product _____. It should be available in about 6 months.

8. I'm so thankful that my teacher _____ so many errors in my writing.

9. I grew up on a farm that raised _____.

Answers

1. under no illusion

2. factory farms

3. come to grips with

4. methane gas

5. transform

6. has a lot of potential

7. in the pipeline

8. overlooks

9. cattle

Talking About a Dissatisfied Customer

Emma and Roxy are talking about a customer, Tony.

Emma: **Word on the street** is that Tony is pretty unhappy with us.

Roxy: Oh that guy? He just wants to make **a quick buck**. He doesn't care about quality and our reputation is **on the line** every time we accept a contract from him.

Emma: Yeah, you need a pretty **thick skin** to work with him. He **shoots from the hip** and almost entirely lacks **self-awareness**!

Roxy: He certainly **keeps us on our toes**. I think we need to **hold our ground** though and not **lower our standards**. That's going to hurt us **in the long run**.

Emma: You're right. He can **take his business elsewhere** if he's so unhappy.

Vocabulary

word on the street: Rumors or news.

quick buck: Making money quickly, often by cutting corners.

on the line: At risk.

thick skin: Ability to not get upset or offended at things.

shoots from the hip: Makes decisions without thinking a lot about them.

self-awareness: Conscious knowledge about oneself.

keeps us on our toes: Always ready to deal with anything that might happen.

hold our ground: Not give way.

lower our standards: Reduce quality

in the long run: Long-term.

take his business elsewhere: Choose another company or person to work with.

Practice

1. I'm afraid that he'll _____ and we'll struggle to make targets.

2. He entirely lacks _____ and it hurts his job performance.

3. She _____ and needs some solid advisors around her because of this.

4. I think we can make a _____ on this during the holiday season.

5. _____, it's better for us to improve efficiency instead of hiring more people.

6. I'm afraid that if we _____, we're going to lose market share.

7. The _____ is that Tony is going to get fired.

8. You have to have a _____ to work with him.

9. Let's _____ on this. We're 100% correct about this.

10. Our jobs are _____ if we can't figure this out.

11. That new client really _____.

Answers

1. take his business elsewhere

2. self-awareness

3. shoots from the hip

4. quick buck

5. in the long run

6. lower our standards

7. word on the street

8. thick skin

9. hold our ground

10. on the line

11. keeps us on our toes

Comprehension Questions

1. According to Emma, what is the current sentiment about Tony among people familiar with their business?
2. How does Roxy describe Tony's approach to business?
3. What qualities does Emma attribute to Tony, suggesting that working with him requires a certain characteristic?
4. How does Emma characterize Tony's communication style?
5. According to Roxy, what is the challenge of working with Tony, and what does she believe the company should do in response?
6. What does Emma agree with Roxy about in terms of dealing with Tony, and what decision does she suggest if Tony remains unhappy?
7. From the dialogue, can you infer any specific actions or behaviors exhibited by Tony that contribute to the challenges discussed by Emma and Roxy?

Answers

1. According to Emma, Tony is pretty unhappy with their company.
2. Roxy describes Tony as someone who wants to make a quick buck and doesn't care about quality.
3. Emma suggests that working with Tony requires a pretty thick skin, indicating that he might be challenging to deal with.
4. She characterizes Tony's communication style as "shooting from the hip" and implies that he almost entirely lacks self-awareness.
5. Roxy believes that, despite the challenges, they need to hold their ground and not lower their standards when dealing with Tony.
6. Emma agrees with Roxy's stance on maintaining standards and suggests that Tony can take his business elsewhere if he remains unhappy.
7. Specific actions or behaviors exhibited by Tony might include prioritizing profit over quality, having a direct and perhaps abrasive communication style, and not being considerate of the impact on the company's reputation.

Discussion Questions

1. How do you think a company should balance the need for revenue and maintaining high standards when dealing with clients who prioritize quick results over quality?

2. In your experience, how does working with challenging clients impact the overall workplace dynamics and the morale of a team?

3. Reflecting on the dialogue, what are some potential consequences for a company's reputation when accepting contracts from clients who prioritize profit over quality? How important is reputation in today's business landscape?

4. From a business perspective, how might a company determine when it's appropriate to hold its ground and maintain high standards, even if it means potentially losing a client?

5. Discuss the role of effective communication in managing relationships with clients who have challenging demands.

Break Up

Carrie: Did you **break up** with Chris yet?

Keith: I was hoping you wouldn't ask me that question! I can't **go through with** it. I'm worried that he's going to be **pissed off** at me.

Carrie: You can **let him off** easily though, right? Be super kind. I know that you don't like **hanging around** with him.

Keith: It's true, yes. I need to **shake things up** and finally end it. Let me go do it right now before I **talk myself out of** it.

Vocabulary

break up: End a romantic relationship.

go through with: Do something that you have planned in advance.

pissed off: Be angry at someone or about something.

let him off: Release.

hanging around: Spending time with.

shake things up: Make a change.

talk myself out of: Convince yourself not to do something.

Practice

1. I think you should _____ with Tony. He's not a good guy!

2. Jay is _____ because I made him clean his room.

3. I have to not _____ asking women out. I just get so nervous

4. Sid and Jen are _____ together a lot these days. Maybe they'll start dating?

5. I'm not sure I can _____ the tattoo. It seems so painful.

6. We need to _____ a bit. Maybe we need to fire one of the low-performers?

7. I'm not sure you should _____ so easily. He needs some punishment for what he did. You don't always need to be the good guy.

Answers

1. break up

2. pissed off

3. talk myself out of

4. hanging around

5. go through with

6. shake things up

7. let him off

No Pain No Gain

Jay and Lily are talking about going back to school.

Jay: I'm thinking about going back to school to study engineering! Hitting the books again. Am I crazy? I haven't been in school for years but I'm so tired of my **dead-end job**.

Lily: Well, as I like to say, "**No pain, no gain**!" If you're going to **make some bank** at a new job afterwards, then why not? You can **reinvent** yourself if you want to.

Jay: That's what I thought too. I'm going to enjoy the **calm before the storm** though. I'm going to be **as busy as a beaver** once the semester starts up in September.

Lily: Oh, you'll **weather the storm** just fine and it'll be **happily ever after** for you. You've got a **good head on your shoulders.** Let's get a beer tonight. You can tell me more about your plan.

Vocabulary

dead-end job: A job without possibility of promotion or advancement

no pain, no gain: Stress and difficulties are to be expected when doing hard work for a goal.

make some bank: To earn lots of money.

reinvent: Make something new again.

calm before the storm: A quiet period before a difficult time.

as busy as a beaver: Working a lot or very hard.

weather the storm: Make it through, or survive a difficult situation.

happily ever after: Go through the rest of your life happily.

good head on your shoulders: Has good common sense, good judgement, is practical.

Practice

1. I'm going to work up in northern Canada to _____.

2. I'm just going to enjoy the _____. Things will get crazy with final exams next month.

4. I'm trying to become an engineer. It's tough going but _____.

5. My husband works at a _____. He says the pay is terrible and they don't give raises.

6. You have a _____. You'll be fine at university.

7. Do you think that Tom and Cindy will be a _____ story?

8. It's going to take more than that to _____.

9. I want to _____ myself with a new job that allows for personal growth.

10. He's _____ with that new course he's taking.

Answers

1. make some bank

2. calm before the storm

4. no pain, no gain

5. dead-end job

6. good head on your shoulders

7. happily ever after

8. weather the storm

9. reinvent

10. as busy as a beaver

Swallow My Pride

Nathan is talking to his friend Zeke about looking for a job.

Zeke: Hey Nathan, how's the **job search** going? Anything going on?

Nathan: Not well. I've been **applying for** jobs but no bites yet. There are so many **job seekers** out there now with the high **unemployment rate**. I might have to **swallow my pride** and take an **entry-level job**. I was hoping for something better but that's not likely now. It's **kind of late in the game**.

Zeke: You could **do an internship**?

Nathan: Nah, I need to **earn money** now. I've got bills to pay with my massive student loans.

Zeke: **Hang in there,** my friend. Any **stable** job isn't a bad thing in this economy.

Vocabulary

job search: The process of looking for a job.

applying for: Seeking employment by sending out applications/resumes/CVs.

job seekers: People who are looking for a job.

unemployment rate: The number of people without jobs measured against the total workforce (listed as a percentage).

swallow my pride: Humble myself.

entry-level job: A job that doesn't require much (or any) experience.

kind of late in the game: Too late in the process to be useful.

do an internship: Work for free to gain experience.

earn money: Make cash.

hang in there: Don't give up.

stable: Secure; not changing.

Practice

1. I want to give up on my _____. I'm not even getting any interviews.

2. _____, okay? I know it's difficult but it'll be worth it when you're done.

3. I had to _____ and apologize to my teacher last week.

4. I'm trying to think of creative ways to _____ this summer.

5. My job isn't _____. I can be laid off at any time.

6. There's a seminar for _____ tomorrow night at the employment center.

7. Sorry, it's not possible. You're _____ for internship applications, aren't you?

8. The _____ is 3.5% in Canada.

9. I think I might _____ to get some experience.

10. Most university graduates take an _____ after they graduate.

11. My goal is _____ at least three jobs a day.

Answers

1. job search

2. hang in there

3. swallow my pride

4. earn money

5. stable

6. job seekers

7. kind of late in the game

8. unemployment rate

9. do an internship

10. entry-level job

11. applying for

Evolution

Lana and Cindy are talking about an article they read about the American education system.

Lana: You wouldn't believe what I read the other day. It was about the **debate** in the USA over what to teach in science classes—**evolution** or **creationism**.

Cindy: I've heard a bit about that. Most other countries **take it for granted** that the **theory** of evolution is a real thing. Not in the USA though. There are many people who **deny** it.

Lana: I know, there's so much evidence for it though. For example, **the fossil record**. Who could deny it? It's not controversial at all!

Cindy: Well, **the driving force** behind it is the Christian Church. They have a lot of **influence** over many spheres of life in the USA, including things like abortion rights.

Lana: I'm not sure why **Joe Public** has so much influence. Scientists should decide what to teach in science class.

Vocabulary

debate: Discussion where people have different viewpoints.

evolution: The theory that humans evolved from earlier forms like apes.

creationism: The theory that God created humans exactly as they are.

take it for granted: Assume that something is true, without questioning it.

theory: A system of ideas to explain something that may, or may not, be true.

deny: Say that something isn't true.

the fossil record: A scientific term. Refers to fossils and the information discovered through them.

the driving force: The power behind something.

influence: Affect someone or something.

Joe Public: The general public's attitude toward a topic (made into a single person).

Practice

1. We can _____ about it all day, but I'm not going to change my mind.

2. You can't _____ that his presentation was excellent, even though you don't like him.

3. Abortion rights. You can't _____ in the USA.

4. How can you not believe in _____? It's clear we descended from apes.

5. You have more _____ with Tony than you think. He always listens to you.

6. In my opinion, evolution isn't a _____. There's so much evidence.

7. I don't care what _____ has to say about it. We need to do the right thing here.

8. The Catholic Church is _____ for many conservative viewpoints in the USA.

9. _____ shows that humans have evolved over millions of years.

10. Many religious people believe in _____.

Answers

1. debate

2. deny

3. take it for granted

4. evolution

5. influence

6. theory

7. Joe Public

8. the driving force

9. the fossil record

10. creationism

154

Talking About Changing Suppliers

Jimmy and Rob are talking about a supplier who is ripping them off.

Jimmy: I'm tired of being **ripped off** by those guys. It's not **cost-effective** for us to use them.

Rob: I know, they don't give us enough **bang for the buck**. They were okay years ago but now companies that make that stuff are **a dime a dozen**. It should be **give and take**, but all they do is take.

Jimmy: Okay, let's **get the ball rolling** on this. But, I want to do everything **by the book** and read through that contract with a **fine-tooth comb** before we take any action.

Rob: Good call. I'll get legal on that **ASAP.** And, start pricing out alternative suppliers.

Vocabulary

ripped off: Got cheated.

cost-effective: Something that offers good value.

bang for the buck: Something that offers good value for the money you paid for it.

a dime a dozen: Common; many options for the same product or service.

give and take: Mutual compromise.

get the ball rolling: Start something.

by the book: Doing something according to the rules.

fine-tooth comb: Reference to thoroughly checking through something.

ASAP: As soon as possible.

Practice

1. Please get back to me _____.

2. I'd love to have a more _____ relationship with them.

3. It's more _____ for us to develop this ourselves.

4. Make sure you go through the small print with a _____.

5. Let's do everything _____ here. The regulators are watching us closely.

6. Coffee shops are _____ in Vancouver.

7. We need to get more _____ from them.

8. Let's _____ on this project. Time is running out.

9. I'm afraid that we're going to get _____. Keep a close eye on them.

Answers

1. ASAP

2. give and take

3. cost-effective

4. fine-tooth comb

5. by the book

6. a dime a dozen

7. bang for the buck

8. get the ball rolling

9. ripped off

Comprehension Questions

1. According to Jimmy, what is his main concern regarding their current supplier?

2. How does Rob describe the value they receive from the current supplier, and what has changed over the years?

3. In Rob's opinion, what should the relationship between their company and the supplier ideally involve, and how does he feel it currently stands?

4. How does Rob respond to Jimmy's suggestion about taking action, and what steps does he propose to address the situation?

5. From the dialogue, what can you infer about the current state of the relationship between Jimmy and Rob's company and their supplier?

6. How might the perceived lack of cost-effectiveness with the current supplier impact the overall profitability and efficiency of Jimmy and Rob's business?

7. In your opinion, how important is it for businesses to regularly evaluate and potentially change their suppliers? What factors should be considered in such decisions?

8. From Rob's response, can you identify the urgency and seriousness with which they plan to address the supplier issue?

Answers

1. According to Jimmy, his main concern is that they are being ripped off by their current supplier, and it's not cost-effective for their company to use them.

2. Rob describes the current supplier as not giving them enough "bang for the buck," suggesting that the value they receive has diminished over the years, possibly due to increased competition.

3. In Rob's opinion, the relationship between their company and the supplier should involve give and take, but he feels that currently, all the supplier does is take.

4. Rob responds positively to Jimmy's suggestion, agreeing that it's a good call. He mentions getting legal involved and starting to price out alternative suppliers.

5. From the dialogue, it can be inferred that the relationship between Jimmy and Rob's company and their supplier is strained due to perceived issues of being ripped off and a lack of cost-effectiveness.

6. The perceived lack of cost-effectiveness with the current supplier may negatively impact the overall profitability and efficiency of Jimmy and Rob's business, potentially leading to financial losses.

7. In evaluating the importance of regularly changing suppliers, it depends on factors such as the competitiveness of the market, changes in the quality or cost-effectiveness of the supplier, and the overall goals of the business.

8. From Rob's response, it can be inferred that they view the issue with the supplier as serious and urgent, as he commits to getting legal involved "ASAP" and initiating the process of finding alternative suppliers.

Discussion Questions

1. In your experience or perspective, how can businesses effectively navigate challenges with suppliers, especially when issues of cost-effectiveness and diminishing value arise?

2. Discuss the importance of regularly reviewing and evaluating supplier relationships in the context of changing market dynamics. How can businesses ensure they are getting the best value from their suppliers over time?

3. From the dialogue, it seems legal considerations play a significant role in addressing issues with the supplier. In your opinion, how crucial is a well-drafted contract in supplier relationships, and what steps can businesses take to ensure contractual clarity and fairness?

4. Reflecting on Rob's comment about companies making similar products being a "dime a dozen," how might increased competition impact the dynamics of supplier relationships for businesses?

5. When faced with concerns about a current supplier, what factors should businesses consider when deciding whether to pursue alternatives?

Before You Go

If you found this book useful, please leave a review wherever you bought it. It will help other English learners, like yourself find this resource.

You might also be interested in these books: *Advanced English Conversation Dialogues* and *The Big Book of Phrasal Verbs in Use*. Both of them are by Jackie Bolen. You can find them wherever you like to buy books. They have hundreds of helpful English phrases and expressions that can be used in a wide variety of situations. Learn to speak more fluently in American English.

Made in United States
Troutdale, OR
02/25/2025

29313696R00091